Journeys with
CELTIC
Christians

Rodney Newman

Abingdon Press
Nashville

Journeys with CELTIC Christians

Rodney Newman

JOURNEYS WITH CELTIC CHRISTIANS
by Rodney Newman

Copyright © 2015 by Rodney Newman

Library of Congress Cataloging-in-Publication Data

Newman, Rodney (Pastor)
 Journeys with Celtic Christians / Rodney Newman. — First [edition].
  pages cm
 Includes bibliographical references.
 ISBN 978-1-63088-981-4 (pbk.)
 1. Celtic Church. 2. Celts—Great Britain—Religion. 3. Celts—Ireland—Religion. 4. Christian pilgrims and pilgrimages. I. Title.
 BR748.N53 2015
 274.1'03—dc23
                        2015024920

15 16 17 18 19 20 21 22 23 24—10 9 8 7 6 5 4 3 2 1
Manufactured in the United States of America

Dedication

To my wife, Ann,
and our children, Carus and Rachel,
whose love and encouragement
fill my heart with joy.

To my parents, Herman and Doris Newman,
whose example of faithful living
continues to nurture me.

To my sister, Towana,
whose honesty and support keep me grounded.

Thanks for sharing the journey.

Contents

Introduction

Every summer when I was a child, my parents would load our little car with suitcases, put my sister and me in the backseat, and take off on our annual vacation. Some of these trips were short hops from our home in northeastern Oklahoma, often to Six Flags in Arlington, Texas. Other journeys stretched for days, such as when we went to Mount Rushmore and Yellowstone and when we drove to San Francisco to visit relatives.

Those road trips are some of the most vivid and happiest memories of my childhood. When I wasn't reading or keeping a list of state license plates we spotted and my sister wasn't sleeping, we were fighting over precious turf defined by the line in the design of the vinyl in the backseat. We spent the night in some rather sketchy places and sometimes picked up bread and bologna in a small-town grocery store and enjoyed a picnic by the side of the road.

Our family didn't have a lot of money, but my parents saved what they could and made judicious choices while on the road. They endured the noise of excited children, which seemed to get louder as the traffic got more intense. I asked my dad one time why they were so persistent in taking us on trips. He said that when he was a child, their family struggled financially. He remembered one of his elementary school teachers describing so vividly to the class the many places she had visited. He ached inside, wanting desperately to experience all those places as well while knowing it was beyond their means. He made a promise to himself that if he ever had children, he would make sure they traveled.

My parents' commitment had a profound influence on me as an adult. I worked for a major airline for six years, which allowed me to see much of the United States. I attended a seminary in the Northeast and spent a summer internship in western Nebraska. While on the staff at Boston Avenue United Methodist Church in Tulsa, I participated in several mission trips to Latin America as well as ones to Slovakia and Russia. My wife and I have continued the tradition and taken our son and daughter to places very different from our home. Travel is in my blood.

It is an essential characteristic of the people of God as well. One of the primary metaphors in the Bible is the journey narrative. This is established clearly when God calls Abram and Sarai to leave their settled home to go to a "land that I will show you" (Genesis 12:1). And they went. We read of the Exodus from Egypt and the wilderness wanderings, of Ruth and Naomi traveling from Edom to Bethlehem, of exile and return. Jesus was born after Mary and Joseph traveled from their home and, as an adult, had "nowhere to lay his head" (Matthew 8:20). Paul's ministry was shaped by a series of voyages over land and sea. There is a restlessness that propels the people of God to explore new worlds and to share the good news with an ever-expanding circle.

Archaeologists tell us that the earliest home of Celtic culture was in Switzerland. From there, it fanned out as far east as central Turkey and Greece and as far west as Spain. The largest population settled in the British Isles and Ireland. Around this same time, the Roman army was pushing the boundaries of their empire, but they never conquered Ireland.

Early missionaries to Ireland faced an unprecedented situation. For the first three hundred years, Christianity was primarily an urban religion; Ireland was completely rural. Traditional models of evangelism were of little help there, so those bearing the gospel chose a very bold and creative response. They listened and learned about the ways of the Celtic people, about their customs and laws, about their holidays and religious expression. They did not require the Celts to become Roman before they could become Christian. The result was an expression of Christianity found nowhere else. Their pre-Christian heritage shaped a faith that was intellectual and mystical, honored the natural world as an expression of God, gave a more prominent role to women, and created liturgical objects known for their beauty and intricate detail.

As their history indicates, travel was in the Celtic blood as well. As we will see, they embarked on physical and spiritual pilgrimages, taking them away from their beloved tribal villages and pushing themselves to explore where the Holy Spirit was leading them.

This is stated most effectively in *The Voyage of Saint Brendan*, a tale written in the tenth century in Ireland that would become one of the most popular texts in Europe during the Middle Ages. The story follows Saint Brendan and a small group of monks who set sail from the western coast looking for the "Promised Land of the Saints." Much like Odysseus, they encounter a number of temptations and dangers along the way. Angry blacksmiths hurl red-hot boulders at them, causing the water to boil. They find an island filled with singing birds whose song they soon recognize as psalms offered in constant praise of God. Just before Easter, they build a paschal fire on what appears to be a small island that they are surprised to learn is actually the back of a great whale! The group travels for seven years, always circling back to the same location each year to celebrate major Christian holidays. When they finally approach the Promised Land of the Saints, they find it shrouded in fog until land suddenly appears. It is a place of beauty beyond compare—flowing rivers and rolling hills with precious stones scattered over the ground as common as rocks. The vegetation is always in fruit and flower that never decay. There is no hunger or thirst or want of any kind. Despite their wishes, the people of the island tell them that they cannot stay, that they must return to their home. As a parting gift, they are allowed to take a few of the precious stones with them.

This story tells us much about the Celtic Christians' understanding of their spiritual journey. For them, time was oriented around the Christian year; its repetition provided a sense of comfort in the midst of changing times and life's storms, and the life of Jesus shaped their own lives. They also understood that their worship was not isolated; their song joined with the whole created order in praising God. It is also interesting that the Promised Land of the Saints was much closer to home than they imagined. They looked far and wide and found it just off the coast where they left. They returned home with tokens of that happy land, reminders of the blessing that awaited, the foretaste of which we now enjoy.

This book invites you to come alongside the Celtic travelers. Allow them to open your heart to the adventures and the challenges of nurturing our spiritual lives in order to be effective witnesses in the world. The first chapter identifies different types of journeys and asks how your journey began and how it can be made even more alive. Chapter 2 explores the Celtic practice of "soul friendship" and looks at ways we can be more intentional about supporting one another in our Christian walk. "Markers on the Journey," the third chapter, focuses on the high-standing stone crosses that still dot the Irish landscape. We'll see how they were used to remember and teach beloved Bible stories and how they marked sacred spaces where God seemed especially close. Extending hospitality to strangers is rooted in many societies, and it was a highly prized practice among the Celtic peoples. Saint Brigid of Kildare will be our guide in Chapter 4, inspiring us with her stories of radical welcome and care. There are some necessary journeys that we do not wish to take: illness, aging, changing schools when parents move. Many who know Saint Patrick only from legends around his holiday in March will be sur-prised how his experience of forced enslavement, harrowing escape, and return to Ireland to share the gospel has much to teach us about making these difficult journeys. That is the focus of Chapter 5. Our journey comes to an end in Chapter 6, appropriately with a benediction—several blessings, in fact, as we read the beautiful Celtic prayers that allow us to see the presence of God in the ordinary events of every-day life.

1

Embarking on the Journey

Embarking on a journey always arouses a degree of anxiety. Even if you can't wait for the adventures ahead, leaving the familiar to enter the unfamiliar raises questions: "What did we forget to pack?" "How will I react if something goes wrong?" "What have we not anticipated?"

These questions become more pressing when traveling with small children. That's what my wife, Ann, and I experienced, anyway, as we went over checklists and buckled everyone into the van for our annual trip to Lake Okoboji in northwestern Iowa. A midway point between our home in Oklahoma and her brother's family in North Dakota, this location provided a beautiful setting for our families to enjoy a fun time reconnecting across the miles.

One of my favorite photographs from those reunions is one of me sitting in a chair overlooking the lake with my daughter, Rachel, two years old at the time, sitting in my lap. We're both very relaxed, with her resting after an active day and me reading a copy of *The Celtic Way*, by Ian Bradley.

At first glance, the photo captures a moment of affection and bonding between father and daughter. What is not evident is the ray of hope shining into my heart in the midst of a time of spiritual turmoil that had been troubling my soul.

For much of my life, I had experienced God as one of guilt and shame, always watching, not so much to care for me but to wait for me to make a mistake. Following the rules, affirming certain beliefs, observing particular practices was what constituted the life of faith. I knew there had to be more. I wanted to love God, not just prevent God from rejecting me. I wanted to experience God, not just claim a correct, if distant, relationship.

Some of my friends had similar yearnings, so we embarked on a journey of discovery. We read theologians outside our particular tradition. We plumbed the stories of faithful Christians in church history who had similar struggles. We challenged one another to dare to listen closely and honestly to our spiritual questions.

One afternoon, my friend Mike and I were sharing our frustrations. No matter how much we tried, all our spiritual efforts never seemed to be enough to please God. It felt as if God always wanted more. At one point in the conversation, seemingly very casually, Mike said, "Maybe we've got this backwards. Everything we've read in the Bible and seen in the witness of other people says that faith starts with God, not us. God's love comes first, before we can do anything to earn it or to reject it. We do good works not in order to *earn* God's love but *in response* to God's love." It was as if a lightning bolt went through me, almost physically knocking me to the floor. The beauty of that truth brought me into the presence of a God I had only dreamed to be true and now was surging through my very being.

Soon I continued exploring the depths of this experience through studies at seminary. The teaching of gifted professors, casual conversations with patient colleagues, and a welcoming environment that allowed me to ask any question were truly medicine for my soul.

Working as an associate pastor enabled me to share with others this wonderful liberation I had found. I loved teaching the Bible, sharing with persons in times of transition and grief, and building a community of service to others. But after a few years, residual echoes of those old struggles started to haunt the edges of my spirit and, increasingly, began moving inside to linger as unwelcome guests. Some of the joy was fading, and questions of faith persisted.

As unlikely as it sounds, Christians from ancient Ireland are the ones who provided the inspiration to restore my faith and who continue to inspire me. I'm not alone. Recent years have seen a revival of interest in Celtic Christianity. The emphasis these Christians placed on community, simplicity of living, and appreciating the presence of God in the natural world speaks to the heart of many persons of faith today. This influence can be seen in liturgies and prayers that reflect a strong devotion to Christ and the awareness of God in the ordinary aspects of life. The great Celtic hymn "Be Thou My Vision" is one of the most popular songs in worship services of various styles. Renewed interest in sensory experiences in worship and personal devotions has inspired more and more individuals to revisit the practices of the early church, such as fixed-hour prayer. The Celtic Christians provide many good models of these practices.

As the church today struggles with connecting to a world that is becoming increasingly secular and socially fragmented, the distinctive characteristics of how Christianity developed among these tribal peoples offer promising lessons on how to reenergize the church.

Who Were the Celts?

A quick Google search of the term *Celt* will confirm what many people today imagine when they hear the word. Medieval warriors with flowing red hair, clad in distinctive tartans, jump off the screen. Maps proudly display the location of ancestral homes in Ireland and Scotland. One usually finds websites advertising pubs or local celebrations of Celtic music and festivals. Soon one runs across New Age symbols and even pagan rituals claiming direct connection to these ancient people.

Those choosing to look beyond popular notions will soon see these for the stereotypes they are, caricatures of a truth of much greater depth. The Celts were a tribal people, preferring to live in villages of around three hundred persons rather than to form any kind of broader kingdom or empire. The men were expected to stay fit, as skirmishes over land and cattle were common. They could be fierce in battle, but most of the time they channeled their energy into caring for their farms with occasional grand celebrations.

Many people are surprised to learn that Celtic tribes actually originated in the area of modern-day Switzerland. Like many ancient people, environmental and political factors pushed them to look for more hospitable locations to set up their homes. Some ventured east where they encountered the Greeks, who called them *Keltoi*, from which we get the term *Celt* (pronounced with a hard *c*). When a large contingent moved into central Turkey, they received another name by which they were identified—*Gauls*. This region became known as Galatia, or the home of the Gauls. Some say that the Galatians addressed in the letter by the apostle Paul in the New Testament were early Celtic people.

The largest movement, however, was to the west. Waves of settlers established so many villages throughout modern-day France that the territory became known as Gaul. They lived happily there for decades until the Romans, led by Julius Caesar, forced them further west onto the British mainland. When the Romans followed them there, the Celts moved to the less desirable rugged Scottish highlands and across the narrow sea to Ireland. While the Romans traded with Irish merchants, they had no interest in conquering the island. The Celts finally found a home—at the edge of the world!

Celtic Christian Distinctives

The first Christians in Ireland were most likely slaves and merchants, primarily in the south where ships for the European continent set sail. Few would have been surprised if Christianity on the island remained confined to small bands of believers for centuries to come. Ireland was a most unlikely mission field. It was so far away from the center of Christendom. The native religion, based around the agricultural cycles with well-established rituals and stories, went back generations and appeared as if it would continue indefinitely.

But by the fifth century, Christianity was making major inroads into the existing culture, defying expectations and established patterns of behavior. What makes the story so fascinating is that the faith would take shape here in a way distinctive from anywhere else in the world. Among the reasons for this, two stand out as key.

First, Ireland was a completely rural island. People lived in small settlements loosely connected to local rulers but for the most part very independent. The first cities would not be established until the ninth century with the coming of the Vikings.

This fact is significant because for the first three hundred years, Christianity was primarily an urban religion. Since we are accustomed to religion being more pronounced in rural areas today, this fact takes many by surprise.

We can see this development in the pages of the New Testament itself. In the Gospel of Luke, Jesus focuses his ministry in the population centers. When we turn the page to the companion volume known as the Book of Acts, we find that the earliest church spread the message in cities. The first Christians were empowered for service on the Day of Pentecost in Jerusalem, and they seemed to be content to stay there until persecutions and the nudging of the Holy Spirit drove them out. When Paul began his missionary journeys, he very deliberately targeted urban areas, especially port cities, sometimes staying as long as two years in one place. One could argue that Paul was seeking the locations where he could make the biggest impact. He could reach more people with the message of the gospel who would then take the good news back to their homes scattered across the known world.

A factor of even greater importance is that people in port cities were more open to hearing different views and more likely to convert should they be so inclined. Think about it. You're living in a little village that generations of your ancestors have called home. You sit down to dinner one evening and announce that you have converted to another religion. After the blank stares, the response might be, "That's fine. Where do you plan to sleep tonight? Where do you plan to live, because you can't stay here." These small social units necessitated conformity in order to survive. Life was too hard, and it took the whole community working in harmony for things to function. They were by nature very conservative places in the sense of maintaining the status quo. The word *pagan* literally means "one from the countryside." Change was frowned upon, at best, if not outright forbidden.

So how does an urban religion evangelize a completely rural society? We will explore this question in more detail in later chapters. For now, suffice it to say that the early missionaries understood that they would have to watch and listen closely to these people, to discover who they were, in order to find a way to communicate the gospel in terms that spoke to their culture.

The second major factor that influenced the shape of Christianity in Celtic lands was that the faith did not come as part of Roman occupation. Up until this point in Western Europe, Christianity came along with, or closely behind, the Roman army. But the Romans didn't conquer Ireland. The faith was not imposed by edict of a king who had converted—there was no imperial monarch in Ireland. You didn't have to become Christian in order to gain promotion in society or success in business. In other words, Christianity didn't come at the point of a sword but through conversation and mutual understanding. As a result, more of the pre-Christian beliefs of the native people continued to influence which aspects of Christianity were emphasized. For example, we find among the Celtic Christians an appreciation for the natural world and the interconnectedness of all creation; an emphasis on blessing other people, even our enemies; the awareness of finding God in the ordinary aspects of life; and the value of relying upon intimate soul friends for the development of the Christian life.

This particular expression of Christianity flourished in the Celtic lands from the fifth through the ninth centuries, then slowly conformed to a style more in line with the majority practices and teachings in Rome.

I don't want to give the impression that there was a "Celtic church." The Christians in Ireland and Scotland worshiped and read the Bible in Latin and understood themselves to be in union with the larger church. Because of the great distance from Rome and their independent spirit, they saw no disparity in promoting theological views and spiritual practices that were a little different from the Roman way. When I speak of "Celtic Christianity," I'm referring to the specific way that the faith developed and was lived in the Celtic lands.

Pilgrimage

While the Celts were not a nomadic people, many exhibited a sense of wanderlust—a restlessness in their makeup—that caused them to strike out on periodic adventures. This is reflected in stories of courageous heroes embarking on excursions where the emphasis was more on the discoveries and challenges of the journey than the destination. Examples include the legendary Bran, who encountered bizarre people and creatures on land and sea, and the great hero Cuchulain, whose supernatural abilities enabled him to defend Ulster against the armies of Connacht.

These stories were cherished, in part, because they described adventures almost unthinkable to the ordinary villager. The gentle rhythms of daily life, familiar voices of loved ones, and stories of beloved ancestors shaped their very identity. The characters in these stories were larger than life, not just in their bravery and skills but in their willingness to risk the loss of their tribal connection, regardless of what fame might be achieved.

Most Celts also had a spiritual connection to the land; it provided food and shelter along with a sense of home, history, and stability. To leave, especially voluntarily, meant letting go of what you held most dear, a decision not to be taken lightly. The hostile landscape and ruffians looking for easy prey made traveling alone unthinkable—it was just too dangerous. A solitary traveler was assumed to be running from something or someone. It was so serious, in fact, that criminals who refused attempts at rehabilitation were punished by being cast adrift on the water with only a day's worth of food, consigned to certain exile and possible death—the worst fate imaginable. Such a person was a *peregrinus*, an alien outside the structure that determined a person's place in society, without rights or protection, an outcast. Separation from home was so painful the Celts even had a word for it, *hiraeth*, meaning "an intense longing or home-sickness."

When Christianity arrived, this somewhat latent urge to travel in the Celtic psyche became an increasingly common practice, so much so that many scholars consider the pilgrimage to be the most distinctive feature of Celtic Christianity.

This was the Celtic manifestation of a common theme among the people of God as embodied in the original pilgrims, Abraham and Sarah. The couple was apparently content with their comfortable lives in Haran. They were established in the community with strong connections and extended family. Their daily routine was set, and their pension plan was in place; in fact, at their age they were already enjoying it. Now there was a rustling to leave. Why? People are often motivated to leave home for wealth, power, or adventure, but Abraham and Sarah appeared to have those things already. The restlessness came from a simple call from God: "Go . . . to the land that I will show you" (Genesis 12:1).

So they went, trekking over the dusty desert that mirrored their own lives—old, barren, landless. When they got to where God was leading them, it appeared that there had been a terrible mistake. Other people were already living in this inhospitable terrain. And it only got worse: They spent the rest of their lives living in tents, with no permanent address. They never got to unpack the china or hang pictures or even feel "at home."

Abraham and Sarah set the template for the people of God. Their saying yes to this incredible call from God to be perpetual pilgrims is what defined them and made them the ancestors of the faithful. They learned things about God and themselves that they would never have discovered staying in their easy chairs in Haran watching TV. In fact, *Haran* means "crossroads," the place of choice.

The Celts immediately saw the story of Abraham and Sarah as their own. As they continued reading, they must have felt that the Hebrew authors were telling their story when they spoke of the Exodus and Exile. The Celts also lived in border regions—between pagan and Christian, male and female, the old gods and festivals and the ones centered on Jesus. They were well aware that they were situated geographically, literally, at the edge of the world. Instead of seeing these liminal, or in-between, places as fraught with danger, they embraced them as times ripe for change and growth.

What better way to give oneself fully to the God they came to know in Jesus than to leave one's native land, to become voluntary *peregrini pro*

Christe, pilgrims for Christ? At first, their eagerness caused them to follow in the spirit of Abraham and Sarah and just strike out for a place they trusted God to show them. Small groups would climb into currachs, boats made of leather wrapped around a wooden frame, and cast themselves from shore, allowing the wind to take them to where they believed God was sending them. It was an act of total faith. They turned up on unknown beaches and wandered the countryside at the mercy of the local inhabitants, living as *hospites mundi*, guests of the world. Some left home never expecting to see it again. Others left for brief periods and would return should the need arise to attend to local or family affairs.

After a while, the purpose of their pilgrimages became more intentional and their motivations more varied. A desire to share the gospel with those who had not heard the message and to establish new churches caused some to travel elsewhere. The Celts were not inclined to build political empires nor villages with large popula-tions. They naturally thought that congregations were meant to be small in number. Once a church got too big for their small building to accommo-date for worship, a group would move on to estab-lish a new congregation. Indeed, this was central to the way the Celts evangelized Scotland and northern England and even onto the European continent.

The Irish love of learning caused them to build libraries and schools of international reputation. European royalty and nobility, and those who aspired to power, had to have a scholar trained in one of these Celtic institutions as the chief teacher for their children.

Regardless of the destination, all these pilgrims saw their physical travels as representing an inner journey as well. They sought to avoid distractions that kept them from focusing on the presence of God. They were searching for their "place of resurrection," a location conducive to spiritual renewal where they would invest their lives and where their mortal bodies would rest until being reunited with their Lord on the last day.

It's obvious that these travels were more than mere sightseeing adventures. These were not pilgrimages in the modern sense of traveling to sacred sites in anticipation of an encounter with the holy. In fact, a designated destination could work against the goal of the experience as is captured in this little verse:

> Who to Rome goes
> Much labour, little profit knows;
> For God, on earth though long you've
>   sought him,
> You'll miss at Rome unless you've
>   brought him.[1]

One did not go in search of God so much as to find a place where the presence of God, already active, could be nourished and expressed in service to others.

Despite all this travel, the old pain of separation from hearth and home persisted. The Celtic Christians described their travels in terms of martyrdom. They read stories of how many of the earliest Christians suffered, even to the point of death, to defend their decision to follow the way of Christ. They admired these accounts of "red martyrdom"— those who spilled their blood rather than renounce their faith in the face of persecution. Although they should have been thankful that Christianity came to Ireland through peaceful means, the lack of true martyrs created a sense that their faith had not been tested, that the spiritual birth had been too easy and, therefore, not as valid as the hard-won heritage of other places. What could they do to prove, if only to themselves, that they were worthy successors to these early heroes and heroines?

In the absence of anyone threatening their physical lives, they interpreted the great sacrifices they were making as particular forms of martyrdom. Enduring the pain of leaving their ancestral homes and abandoning everything they loved for the sake of Christ was a true test of faith, one they called "white martyrdom." Some were content with moving down the road, while others had to feel the pinch of real sacrifice. These brave souls sought out remote places, such as Skellig Michael, the rocky island of steep peaks off the southwest coast of Ireland, or Iona, a small Scottish island that to visit, even in modern times, requires an arduous voyage. The thrill and anxiety of undertaking such a journey is captured in these verses known as Saint Brendan's Prayer:

> Shall I leave the soft comforts of home,
>   O Lord,
> and be without money, power, and
>   honour?

Shall I launch my little boat on the great
    sparkling ocean,
and go on my own on the deep?
Shall I leave the prints of my knees
on my own native land
and face the lonely sea?
Stand by me, God,
when it comes to the wild waves.[2]

But not everyone could just take off from commitments at home, regardless of how much their
hearts yearned to do so. What they could do, however, was to make the same level of commitment
to following the way of Christ as those who had the
opportunity to leave. Their quest was more internal
as they sought freedom from thoughts and behavior that pushed them away from God by observing
such practices as fasting, regular prayer, and offering their labor as a gift to the divine. "Green martyrdom" then was an intentional, voluntary giving up
of normal securities for the sake of trusting fully in
Christ.

For the Celts, being a Christian was synony-
mous with being on a journey. Physical movements, whether achieved through traveling great
distances or through hands lifted in prayer, were
visible signs of an inward and spiritual grace.
There was no such thing as a "static" faith, a belief
or particular spiritual experience trapped in amber
to be admired as a museum artifact or relic. Just as
the first Christians were known as people who followed Jesus on "the Way," so the Celtic Christians
were always attuned to where the Spirit would
lead them next. This was not for the weak of heart.

Embarking on such a journey meant that you would meet strangers with different points of view, that doubt would inevitably arise in the dark valleys, and that the road would venture into questionable neighborhoods—all sources of potential danger, but the very places where the risen Christ promised to be present to invite us into abundant life.

Our Spiritual Journeys

We know about journeys. I've heard that Americans now move their place of residence, on average, every five years. This certainly rings true in our family. While I lived in only two houses in the same city as a child, as an adult I have lived in apartments, dormitories, houses, and parsonages in four states. Our son has lived in four houses in three cities before moving to another residence in college. Even those who haven't moved much geographically have made other transitions, such as from elementary to middle school to high school and college. Some have gone through changes in their jobs, switching careers and moving into retirement. All relationships have their ups and downs along the way: marriage and divorce, breakups and reconciliations, empty nests. Famines and political unrest force thousands of refugees from their homes every year. Many walk the path of recovery from addiction and other illnesses of the body and mind. And our way of thinking can change when what we thought we "knew" to be true is challenged.

The same is true for our nation and culture. We all are learning to navigate the new world of rapid technological innovation that is changing communication, education, our relationships, and even our spirituality. We encounter more cultural diversity and redefinition of sexual expression than ever before. It's easy to feel a little lost—cast adrift—on the many journeys that intersect our lives.

When in your life have you been a pilgrim? When have you struck out from the familiar, either by choice or by circumstance, and found a new world and new relationships?

My journey started in a rather strict church in a small town. Their world was clearly defined by bright boundaries of right and wrong with a great deal of pressure to conform to the expectations of that particular community. But from an early age, something stirred within me. While trying to fit in, I always had one eye on the horizon, wondering what might be over the next hill. Through encounters with a number of loving people and a fortunate series of experiences, I was accepted as a student at Princeton Seminary.

Intuitively I felt the need to venture forth from the plains of Oklahoma, from my little corner of God's earth, to explore the broader world. So as autumn approached, I loaded up my boat, which looked very much like a Honda hatchback, and pointed it east to see where God, and the wind, would take me. My friend Craig rode with me for company, but he would be returning by bus after a couple of days. It was on the second evening of our journey that we arrived at the school and found my dormitory. After locating someone to check me in to my room, Craig and I went to a local diner for a late dinner, a little comfort food. I still remember the overwhelming sense of loneliness that took away my appetite. New Jersey seemed so far away from everything that was familiar: The people talked differently, the landscape looked different, and I knew no one there. Later, Craig told me that he was just waiting for me to turn the car around and say, "Let's go back home."

But I stayed. It wasn't long before the adventure of the pilgrimage occupied my attention and shaped my soul. I made friends with classmates from Savannah, Georgia, and Goldsboro, North Carolina; washed dishes with students from Nepal and Kenya; discussed our common calling to ministry with women colleagues; and plunged into the depths of Christian history and experience. I was forever changed. It was there that I found the courage to move to a new home in The United Methodist Church, where I found a sense of self-confidence in facing down old personal challenges, and where I articulated the longings that had been there all along and found renewal through new encounters with God and with others.

Even when the thrill of adventure promised by a spiritual pilgrimage tugs at our hearts, taking that first step can be the most difficult part. We want to take the plunge, but there are just too many loose ends to tie up, too many commitments already made. Perhaps we've started before, only to end up back where we started, more disappointed than if we had never left in the first place. If we could just forget the past and start fresh, we would be ready to go—or so we tell ourselves.

But if we wait for the perfect time, it will never come. The late noted preacher John Claypool observed that we all want to believe that we start our lives at the beginning. But the truth is that we all begin in the middle; each of us is born into a family drama well underway, already shaped by decisions made by people long before we arrived and over which we had no control. We try to impose order by blaming the less-than-perfect people who raised us or by separating the world into neat categories of good and evil. But such simplistic attempts only leave us alienated and frustrated. We have to admit that our lives are lived in the midst of complexity and great ambiguity. In order to move forward, we have to celebrate the good that has been given to us and forgive what we cannot forget, because the string of human brokenness goes so far back, there is no condemnation. We have to let those who came before us, and ourselves, off the hook so that we are able to push off from the shore to live into the new day that God has created and is creating.

Claypool illustrates this with a story from his own family history:

> My great-grandfather had a pear tree
> in the side yard in southern Kentucky
> that I'm told he loved and for years
> and years had harvested, eaten its
> fruit, sat under its shade, and found
> it to be a wonderful companion. One
> night a windstorm came through. When
> he went out, lo and behold, that pre-
> cious pear tree had been blown over,
> uprooted. It was obviously gone. The
> story is that he wept genuine tears
> because of the loss of something that

was very precious. And then an old neighbor came down the road, stood with him in his tears as he lamented the thing that had happened, and then he allegedly asked my great grandfather, "What are you going to do now?" And that hearty old pioneer said, "I'm going to pick the fruit and burn what's left." I'm going to extract from this situation the good that is still there, and then I'm going to relinquish the rest of it into great mercy.[3]

It's always a good time to draw inspiration from the Celtic Christians and go on a spiritual pilgrimage, but there are times in our lives when taking such a step is exactly what's needed. When we feel apathetic or complacent, it's time to launch out to rekindle the passion of faith. When we become too settled, too certain, it's time to launch out of the familiar to be challenged by the views of others and to walk the path of humility to an even richer life. When our world becomes too small, it's time to launch out to explore that which is bigger than ourselves.

One February, I found myself in Ulyanovsk, Russia, located on the Volga River, 550 miles east of Moscow. Our team had been staying in homes of local residents for about a week as we explored ways of supporting nascent Methodist ministries there. My host family had been most gracious to share their small apartment and their delicious meals with me. The language and cultural differences had not felt like obstacles as much as invitations to share our respective views of the world and our common hope for better days ahead. On the morning of our departure, I packed my suitcase, made one last check to make sure I had everything, and started out the front door. My hosts very politely but firmly pulled me back into the room, closed the door, placed my suitcase beside it, and indicated that I should sit on top of my bag. That's when I noticed that the family had already brought chairs into the same area upon which they promptly sat. For a couple of minutes, we all just sat there, saying nothing, doing nothing, just sitting. Then, as if by prearranged signal, they got up and opened the door. I had to know what just happened. "There's an old Russian custom," they told me, "that before one begins a long journey, just before you leave, you sit in silence. You think about the place you have been, the experiences you have encountered, the people you have met. You give thanks for how they have changed you and remember them so that they go with you on your journey."

A modern Celtic blessing launches courageous pilgrims in a similar fashion:

> May the peace of the Lord Christ go
>   with you,
> wherever He may send you.
> May He guide you through the
>   wilderness,
> protect you through the storm.
> May He bring you home rejoicing
> at the wonders He has shown you.
> May He bring you home rejoicing
> once again into our doors.[4]

2

Friends on the Journey

My wife and I had just received some disturbing news. She was pregnant with our first child. Due to her age and other factors, she was considered high-risk. The doctor had ordered some blood tests to check on a few things. A couple of days later, the phone call came. There was an indicator that the baby might have a health disorder.

Fear, anxiety, and uncertainty about the future all welled up inside us. We tried to console each other, but we shared the same pain and needed an outside voice to offer a comforting word. It seemed too early to alarm our family unnecessarily, so we called Sylvia.

Before we started dating, my wife and I each had developed a friendship with Sylvia. In fact, that common bond eased our transition into married life. Sylvia and some other friends hosted a wedding shower for us, and she knew each of us well enough to enable our relationship to grow through wise counsel.

I first met Sylvia when I became an associate pastor at her church. She had been an active lay-person all her life, and I found her experience and enthusiasm to be very helpful. She also possessed a big personality and could be outspoken and opinionated, so not everyone shared my appreciation. In conversation she would sometimes overwhelm you with words until you finally gave up and went with her "suggestion." But in fairness, when I would respond with a different proposal, she was open to seeing things another way and would become that idea's biggest supporter.

So after receiving the unsettling news about our baby, we thought of Sylvia. Here was someone we both trusted and who had walked through dark valleys with us before. When she answered the phone, we put her on speaker, explained the situation, then sat back, emotionally and spiritually exhausted.

She listened with quiet patience until we were ready for her to respond. Her gentle voice acknowledged our pain and hers. She calmed our fears by reassuring us of the presence of God and that our family of faith would walk with us regardless of what lay ahead. She was detached enough to help us see the bigger perspective—that this was not the end of the world and that we would get through this together.

Soul Friendship

The Christians of early Ireland would say that Sylvia was acting as our "soul friend." The Gaelic word is *anamcara* (*anam* = soul, *cara* = friend). Each member of the faith community had another person who had the specific function of serving as a guide on the spiritual journey. This was not the same role as a modern-day therapist or even a friend to go to for advice about personal problems. Those in an anamcara relationship were focused on how the other was progressing in their walk with God, on how they were feeding their souls in healthy ways, and on challenging them to renew their spirits in times of weakness.

While the Celts made this a major emphasis, the idea of caring for souls has deep historic roots. The earliest Christians were renowned for their care for one another. Even in the pages of the New Testament, we see how some of those who followed Jesus were persecuted for their decision and were alienated from their regular systems of support. So they assembled together and looked after one another in love.

The letter from James, in particular, is concerned with how to nurture a healthy Christian community and the spiritual well-being of individuals within it. James knew how jealousy and lack of mutual respect could cause division among the group. He asks the faith community to consider how they will handle those who succumb to sickness or engage in sinful actions. Will they isolate them so as not to drag everyone else down? Will they be too lenient so as to enable other destructive behavior?

James addresses these very questions. "Are any among you sick? They should call for the elders of the church and have them pray over them, anointing them with oil in the name of the Lord" (James 5:14). The elders, as representatives of the whole body, will not blame the sick person or alienate them. Instead, they will surround them with love and care. When a member sins, those not caught up in the sin are to take the initiative, go to the one in trouble, and invite that person back into the community. In fact, it would be a good idea for everyone to confess their sins to each other continually so as not to stray too far from the fold.

For much of the early days of the church, confession tended to be done publicly. A person stood in front of the congregation and listed all the ways he or she had fallen short of God's intention. You can see how this would lead to great accountability, but it also served as a deterrent to admit to sins in front of the whole community. Fear of shaming encouraged people to keep their sins bottled up inside, cutting them off from the opportunity for healing and growth.

It was in the Egyptian desert, of all places, where this public practice took a turn to a more intimate, personal encounter. Some Christians in Middle Eastern cities grew tired of all the noise and ceaseless activity. They wanted to get away from it all in order to find a place for quiet reflection and the ability to devote their lives to prayer.

Some lived as hermits, coming together with other people only on rare occasions. Most lived in small communities, often sharing a cell, or small living space, with one other person.

After a while, the larger church began to notice these persons who had dedicated themselves to austere lives in the middle of nowhere. They became renowned for their spirituality and closeness to God. Collections of sayings of these desert fathers and mothers illustrate their wisdom in keeping focused on what is essential for spiritual growth and avoiding distractions that would lead to selfishness. They generally appeared as short stories documenting how they taught through word and example:

> A brother asked Abba Poemen, "Some brothers live with me; do you want me to be in charge of them?" The old man said to him, "No, just work first and foremost, and if they want to live like you, they will see to it themselves." The brother said to him, "But it is they themselves, Father, who want me to be in charge of them." The old man said to him, "No, be their example, not their legislator."[1]

There are also stories of the dangers of becoming too serious or narrowly focused:

> Once Abbot Anthony was conversing with some brethren, and a hunter who was after game in the wilderness came upon them. He saw Abbot Anthony and the brothers enjoying themselves, and disapproved. Abbot Anthony said: Put an arrow in your bow and shoot it. This he did. Now shoot another, said the elder. And another, and another. The hunter said: If I bend my bow all the time it will break. Abbot Anthony replied: So it is also in the work of God. If we push ourselves beyond measure,

the brethren will soon collapse. It is
right, therefore, from time to time, to
relax their efforts.[2]

One person greatly influenced by his visit to
the desert was John Cassian. This brilliant, spiritual man from Eastern Europe, perhaps of Celtic
lineage, paid close attention to how the people
in these communities related to God and to one
another. He noticed the importance of the *syncel-
lus*, or "one who shares a cell," with the other. This
close relationship encouraged them to a mutual
practice of *exagoreusis*, "to open the heart," leading
to *hesychia*, "serenity of heart."

Achieving this level of trust allowed them to
share their deepest selves honestly, without fear
of being shamed or discounted by the other, and
promoted equality before Christ. The shift from
public to private confession opened a space that
encouraged vulnerability and honesty. This spiritual
intimacy built on trust formed such close relationships that time or distance could not sever them.
As Cassian wrote,

> There is one kind of love which is indis-
> soluble, where the union is owing not
> to the favour of a recommendation,
> or some great kindness or gifts, or the
> reason of some bargain, or the necessi-
> ties of nature, but simply to similarity of
> virtue. This, I say, is what is broken by
> no chances, what no interval of time or
> space can sever or destroy, and what
> even death itself cannot part.[3]

I suppose the closest I have come to a "sharing-a-cell" relationship was during my first year at seminary. My new friends, Billy and Tripp, and I were single and lived in the dormitories. All three of us were overwhelmed by the challenges of graduate school and concerned about how we would respond. So with heart rates elevated, we filed into our first class, "Introduction to Old Testament Studies," along with the other 124 first-year students. The professor ascended onto the stage, took his place behind the podium, and in his West Texas drawl began: "I have to admit that I am among those who are concerned about grade inflation. So I want you to know upfront how I intend to grade your papers. If you turn in a paper that meets all the expectations, it's a C. If your paper shows particular insight and promise, it's a B. If I wish I had written it myself, it's an A." The lush, green forests of central New Jersey suddenly felt very much like the Egyptian desert.

Finding our footing in that course proved difficult. The three of us compared class notes, discussed the readings, and tried to understand the meaning of the comments on our papers, not to mention the grades we received. Finally the end was in sight. After completing the final exam, we took a walk uptown to unwind. Passing a newsstand, one of us noticed the headline on a tabloid, "Preacher Explodes During Sermon." The story was about "the most bizarre case of spontaneous combustion ever!" when a preacher in Germany suddenly burst into flames before the eyes of his horrified congregation.

It was just the comic relief we needed to release all the pent-up stress. We laughed for days about this wild tale we knew to be fiction but somehow felt like a metaphor for what we had just endured the previous three months. Now that we had time to reflect, we realized that we had done more than study together. We had opened our souls to each other. We were vulnerable enough to admit not knowing all the answers while fanning into flame the passion each of us had to expand our faith in ways we could only dream to be possible.

I realize now our professor that fall day was speaking in the spirit of a caring abbot, not to intimidate, but to offer us an invitation. He knew the wisdom that had been entrusted to his care to pass on to us was too important. Doing the minimum might fill our heads with the right answers, but it wouldn't ignite our hearts by brushing up against the living God. I suspect he knew he was leading us into the desert all along.

> Abbot Lot came to Abbot Joseph and said: Father, according as I am able, I keep my little rule, and my little fast, my prayer, meditation and contemplative silence; and according as I am able I strive to cleanse my heart of thoughts: now what more should I do? The elder rose up in reply and stretched out his hands to heaven, and his fingers became like ten lamps of fire. He said: Why not be totally changed into fire?[4]

The Desert Comes to Ireland

It wasn't long before some of the people influenced by these Christians from the East began traveling west. Cassian established himself in France, and from there his writings spread even further west to Ireland, where they met a receptive audience. The Celts already emphasized community and were prone to a more mystical understanding of spiritual affairs. Trusted counselors were part of the culture before the arrival of Christianity, so the idea of soul friends seemed custom-made for these folks.

Like so many other ideas received from the broader Christian world, they made this practice their own. In Ireland, anamcara relationships might be between persons living in the same village or miles apart. They could be between persons of the same or the opposite gender, between an older and a younger person, or between one belonging to a religious order and a layperson.

The idea of a solo Christian, without involvement in a worshiping community, was inconceivable to them. Everyone needed another person to hear their concerns and for the other to be mindful to correct them when they strayed from the path. For Saint Brigid, "anyone without a soul friend is like a body without a head; is like the water of a polluted lake, neither good for drinking nor for washing."[5]

Depending on geographic proximity, soul friends may have met anywhere from once a year to every few weeks. The quality of the time spent together and the depth of openness determined the nature of the connection. Both parties had to be committed to the goal of creating "soul space" where they could be vulnerable with each other and allow their spirits to breathe. Clear expectations were needed to make sure that someone did not use this bond as an opportunity to exploit the other person or to avoid difficult issues by allowing the conversation to become a gossip session. The most effective anamcara relationships shared specific characteristics.

Accountability

There seemed to be something in the Celtic DNA that caused them to pour everything they had into life. They fought hard, feasted robustly, and took great pride in their work. They brought this same attitude to their faith. If you were going to be a Christian, it was worth doing it well. The anamcara was there for comfort, yes, but also to motivate and encourage constant dedication to spiritual practices. The value of accountability partners is acknowledged today by the many who testify that it is easier to stay on a healthy diet or to maintain an exercise routine if they engage in that practice with someone else. They think twice before reaching for a second cookie if they know someone will be asking them what they had to eat.

The life of a Christian, then, involved much more than a profession of faith. Early Christians were expected to live out their faith through practices such as praying on a regular basis, showing hospitality to strangers, and fasting in certain seasons. The discipline necessary to observe these external actions applied equally to nurturing the internal attitudes of heart and mind.

Developing one's spiritual life is not rocket science. The attempt to make it very complicated often is really an excuse to avoid doing what we know we need to do. Saint Ita established an influential monastery in County Limerick in the sixth century. Her reputation for holiness of life and generosity of spirit attracted many talented young people to spend time in her presence. Such a large number of these protégés went on to become noted leaders that she has been called "the foster mother of the saints of Ireland." Once, Saint Brendan asked Saint Ita the three things most pleasing to God. She answered, "True faith with a pure heart; a simple, spiritual life; and generous acts of charity." When he asked her the three things God hates the most, she replied, "A scowling face, obstinacy in wrong-doing, and too great a confidence in the power of money."[6] Direct and to the point. It's difficult to explain that away.

In the eighteenth century, John Wesley, the founder of the Methodist movement in England, adapted this idea of soul friendship in his class meetings. Small groups of people agreed to gather on a regular basis and to hold each other accountable in love for their spiritual development. They would ask such questions as, "Did the Bible live in me today?" "Do I pray about the money I spend?" "Am I defeated in any part of my life?" While these were not one-on-one relationships, the idea of mutual accountability and a single focus on spiritual development continued the spirit of the Celtic anamcara.

At the heart of the class meetings were three simple rules, reminiscent of Saint Ita. Wesley called them the General Rules by which people gave evidence of their desire for salvation:

> *First*: By doing no harm, by avoiding evil of every kind. . . .
> *Secondly*: By doing good; by being in every kind merciful after their power; as they have opportunity, doing good of every possible sort, and, as far as possible, to all. . . .
> *Thirdly*: By attending upon all the ordinances of God; such are:
> The public worship of God.
> The ministry of the Word, either read or expounded.
> The Supper of the Lord.
> Family and private prayer.
> Searching the Scriptures.
> Fasting or abstinence.[7]

More recently, these rules have been put in more contemporary language by Bishop Rueben Job: Do no harm, do good, and stay in love with God.[8]

A few months ago, I was invited by some colleagues to join with them in a small accountability group. At first I was skeptical. My participation in similar groups in the past felt too structured and judgmental, although I will admit that may have been coming more from my own perceptions than from the other members of the group.

At any rate, I agreed to attend the first meeting to see if maybe this one would be different. I was not disappointed. The process for this group centered on the modern version of Wesley's General Rules. Each of us was asked to list particular ways that we would follow each of the three directives. The purpose was not to find ways that all of us would commit to as a group, but rather that each of us would identify what we felt was needed for where we were on our journey. So I had to think: (1) Where am I currently doing harm? Are there relationships I'm neglecting? Am I being wasteful with the resources entrusted to me so as to harm the earth? (2) What good am I neglecting to do? Are there people I take for granted who should be praised? Am I caring for those on the margins of our society in tangible ways? (3) How have I been nurturing my relationship with God? Am I faithful in worship and prayer? Am I mindful of God's blessings throughout the day, or do I take too many of them for granted? That exercise alone brought me to a new level of accountability.

I am happy to report that subsequent sessions have allowed me to experience firsthand the "soul space" prized so highly by the Celtic anamcaras. The members of the group have created an environment where I can confess my failings knowing that I will receive support, not judgment, in return. I've learned that even when I didn't accomplish a particular goal, the process itself has made me more aware of how I move through the day as a person of faith and that I do so with much more intentionality.

Mutuality

The society of ancient Ireland was not as hierarchical as many others of the time, but there were certainly different classes—slaves, nobles, and crafts persons. Penalties under the law were determined by a person's "honor price" reflecting their status. Every person was well aware of the power inequality exerted and how that dictated their behavior. But when it came to soul friendships, the playing field was to be level. Everyone was susceptible to erring from the path, and all needed guidance. Importing social differences into these relationships would deny the love of Christ given equally to all, without regard to station.

They drew inspiration for this mutuality from a story from the desert tradition featuring the two most prominent hermits of the period. As Christian priest and scholar Jerome tells it, one day Antony, somewhat of a celebrity in his time, was feeling rather proud of what he had given up to follow Christ, so much so that he thought that there was no better monk than himself dwelling in the desert. But in the quietness of the night, it was revealed to him that deep in the desert, there was indeed another monk who was far better and that he should hurry to visit him. So the old man made his way across the scorching sands to be greeted warmly by Paul of Thebes, who had been living in the desert many years before Antony arrived. After exchanging pleasantries, they visited about the state of the world, both political and spiritual. As they talked, they noticed that a crow had settled on a branch of a nearby tree; then it gently flew down and dropped a whole loaf of bread before their wondering eyes. After giving thanks, there was an awkward moment of who should break the bread. Paul insisted that his new friend should have the honor since he was the guest. Antony countered that it was Paul's prerogative by right of seniority. After a while they agreed that each should take hold of the loaf and pull it at the same time—they would share the honor.

We know the Celtic Christians loved this story. The scene is etched into the stone of some of the high-standing crosses across Ireland. It embodies the value of mutual friendship that transcends differences of age and geography. Grudges are not held, and there is ample opportunity for repentance. At the center is the loaf of bread, symbolizing the gift of the Eucharist as well as the companionship of a shared meal.

The Celts also appreciated this same theme in the doctrine of the Trinity as it came to them from the Eastern church. The Greek word to represent this understanding is *perichoresis*, literally meaning "a dance around" (*peri* = around, *choresis* = dance). The relationship among the members of the Trinity—Father, Son, and Holy Spirit—is not static and hierarchical but rather a creative interplay. There is constant motion, always with deference to the others. This image of God served as a model for the Christian community as well.

Self-Awareness

In premarital counseling sessions, I visit with the couple about handling conflict. I usually ask them to think back to when they were children and how the significant adults in their lives handled conflict. Did they fight in front of the children? Was there a lot of yelling and crying, or did they just not talk to each other for a while? I raise this because we tend to think that what we experienced as children is "normal." If you are in a relationship with a person who had a different experience, there could easily be some miscommunication of what is really going on. We then explore a variety of healthy ways to handle conflict, and I encourage them to understand how the other person perceives their disagreements.

I go on to discuss with them how fights in intimate relationships very rarely are about what they appear to be. These conflicts always are rooted in an emotion. It's what I call the "loose thread" theory. If someone is upset over something their partner did or didn't do, they often start fighting over whatever that is. That may fix the problem temporarily, but it will recur time after time. For instance, when someone is upset about the other not taking out the trash (again), or if they were late for dinner (again), you need to regard that as a loose thread. It's an indicator that something is wrong, but it's not what's really at issue. You have to follow that back until you get to an emotion: concern about being disrespected, fear of abandonment, and so forth. You have to deal with the emotional issue at stake; otherwise it will manifest itself in a thousand ways, and the relationship gets caught in an endless loop.

This is true for anyone, not just couples. I remember one day a few years ago, driving down a beautiful tree-lined avenue in the bright sunshine, feeling anything but sunny inside. The car in front of me was moving too slowly, and when they turned without signaling, I almost snapped! That was the moment I had enough sense to grab the loose thread. My anger at this innocent person was way out of proportion to the stimulus. Their driving was not the issue. I had to figure out why I was so angry.

All of us carry emotions and perspectives as a result of past experiences or just due to our personality traits. If we wish to be able to be a soul friend to another person, we have to be self-aware enough not to project our baggage onto the other. If they are struggling with something we have already been through, we can't assume that the way we resolved the issue will be the same remedy for them. If particular theological perspectives have caused me pain, I have to put that aside enough to be able to honor the journey of the other person. While the specifics differ, all of us have been wounded in some way. We serve others by tapping into that woundedness in a manner that enables us to understand the pain of the other, not by imposing our wounds on them.

Medicine for the Soul

The good citizens of Rome in the late fourth century had seen a lot, but nothing prepared them for the man who was shaking up the church and the community. Pelagius, a large, boisterous, charismatic Celt, had come to town from his home in the western lands and was appalled at the lax moral standards he witnessed there. And he wasn't quiet about it. He publicly called out those living self-indulgent lifestyles, made more apparent when contrasted with his own disciplined life. He engaged in untraditional actions by Roman standards, such as teaching women to read. It seemed he had a knack for alienating just about everyone. Jerome spoke for many when he dismissed Pelagius as "a most stupid fellow, heavy with Irish porridge."

What got Pelagius in real trouble, however, was the war of words he entered into with Augustine over the issue of human nature and free will. In observing the pervasiveness of sin in the world, Augustine proposed that this was due to what has been called in the Western church "original sin." Focusing on the disobedience of Adam and Eve recorded in Genesis 3, he asserted that their sin is transferred to every human being from that time forward. Everyone is born in sin and must be redeemed by the grace of God. Pelagius, in contrast, preferred to start reading at the beginning of Genesis, where the work of each day of Creation—the sun and stars, plants, animals, human beings—all are declared good since they originate with God. Every person then, as a child of God, is born with that essential goodness. He acknowledged the pervasiveness of sin in the world and that every person falls under its influence very early, but each person is responsible for his or her own sin; they don't begin bearing the stain due to the actions of others.

Pelagius held very extreme views. He believed, for instance, that since we got ourselves into the mess of sinfulness, we could get ourselves out. His later followers, however, including John Cassian, knew that we cannot save ourselves, that we need the grace of God to break the bonds of selfishness and alienation.

That grace comes to us in the person of Jesus Christ—the revelation of God in the world. By his teachings and his actions, Jesus embodied the ideal of what God had in mind for humanity from the very beginning. He confronted the evil forces of darkness that separate us from God and from one another, and he now liberates us to walk as children of light. Jesus choosing to die on the cross was the ultimate expression of the lengths to which God will go to enter into suffering with us—the greatest act of love.

In the Celtic understanding, salvation is not a matter of changing human beings into different people, from worthless to worthy. Salvation is the restoration, or a recovery, of the person God created us to be in the first place.

Sin, then, that which separates us from God and our true selves, was not seen as a crime to be punished; rather, sin represented a wound or an illness that needed to be healed. That change in perspective was the key that made soul friendships possible. Punitive language was better suited for the secular law courts where prescribed punishments were matched with specific crimes. But in matters of the spirit, each person, each situation was different. Through discerning conversation and questions, a gifted anamcara would spend time diagnosing the spiritual problem, then develop a remedy by which the person could find a cure. They would prescribe "medicine for the soul" that would address the symptoms and the disease.

The treatments varied according to the need. Sometimes they suggested that the person develop a discipline directly opposite of their confessed sin. For instance, a person struggling with greed would be instructed to practice specific acts of generosity; for gluttony, a period of fasting was prescribed. Others would need to make restitution to victims of their hurtful behavior and seek reconciliation with the larger community.

Salvation is a process. There might be particular moments of decision to follow the way of Christ and occasional times of spiritual ecstasy, but the goal is to grow into the image of Christ. This is always a work in progress; the important thing is that we continue moving toward the goal. The New Testament calls this process "sanctification." Martin Luther spoke of it as a life of repentance. John Wesley referred to it as being made perfect in our love of God and each other.

Becoming like Christ is not a reward we earn or something we can achieve on our own. We need friends—to hold us accountable, to show us a way forward when there appear to be no options, to comfort us in times of loss. But most importantly, we need someone to remind us that we are first and foremost children of God. Come to think of it, this is what Jesus did in his ministry on earth. Whenever he encountered someone who had been pushed to the margins, he never addressed them according to the label society had placed on them: "leper," "prostitute," "annoying child," "sick woman," "tax collector." Instead, he always saw them and spoke to them as the persons God created them to be. He addressed their potential, not their past. And in that act alone, they were healed.

Author Anne Lamott made her commitment to the Christian life after years struggling with addiction and brokenness. Now active in her Presbyterian church outside San Francisco, she offers compelling insights into our faith.

She writes about one morning teaching the youngest Sunday school class at her church, children ages 3–6. They began the class with an activity called "Loved and Chosen":

> I sat on the couch and glanced slowly around in a goofy, menacing way, and then said, "Is anyone here wearing a blue sweatshirt with Pokémon on it?" The four-year-old looked down at his chest, astonished to discover that he matched this description—like, What are the odds? He raised his hand. "Come over here to the couch," I said. "You are so loved, and so chosen." He clutched at himself like a beauty pageant finalist. Then I asked if anyone that day was wearing green socks with brown shoes, a Giants cap, an argyle vest? Each of them turned out to be loved and chosen, which does not happen so often. Even Neshama (my fellow teacher)—Anyone in red shoes today?—leapt toward the couch with relief.

What Anne Lamott describes is nothing less than the goal of every soul friendship: to create a safe place where we can name our fears, share our sadness, know that we are loved and chosen, and become the persons God created us to be.[9]

3

Markers on the Journey

I t was a cool, overcast morning, not unusual for Ireland in June. Our group of twelve from Oklahoma City University was beginning the fifth day of a two-week trip to study Celtic Christianity in the land of its birth. This day, however, would take us back in time—before the arrival of the Christians, even before the Celts moved into the land.

About thirty miles north of Dublin, near the River Boyne, stands a mound of earth and stone built over five thousand years ago—older, in fact, than the great pyramids in Egypt. This structure, known today as Newgrange, is the finest example of passage tombs scattered around the Atlantic seaboard of Europe. Although the style varies, these earthen mounds have a door cut in one side leading to an inner chamber.

Even by modern standards, Newgrange is an impressive sight. Our group had never seen anything like it. We walked around the white quartz and granite walls covering about an acre and imagined the possible meaning of boulders etched with spiral motifs. The small interior room can accommodate only a few visitors at a time, so we wedged our way around the narrow opening in the rocks and stood shoulder to shoulder in the dank enclosure. Our guide explained that scholars weren't sure of the purpose of these structures, but many believe they were used in rituals to transport the souls of those who had recently died to the spirit world.

What they do know is that Newgrange was situated very specifically so that on the winter solstice, the rising sun would shine directly into the doorway. Our guide explained that in order for us to visualize this, an artificial light had been installed to simulate the experience. After warning us, she turned off the lights. We stood in pitch dark, buried in the earth, straining for the slightest glimmer of light. And suddenly, there it was. It was only a narrow beam, but it slowly made its way down the passage, dissecting our group, then finally illuminating the back wall. We could only wonder what motivated these early builders to commit the effort and resources of the entire community to create this dramatic effect. It was surely of utmost importance to who they were as a people.

Every culture shapes its identity by the way its people choose to tell time and the way they organize their space. In order to know where we are, we need markers that orient us within a community, on a road, or in our life cycle.

Our sense of well-being is determined in large part by our perception of orientation in space and time. When motoring along an interstate highway, we watch for signs indicating the distance to our

destination and count down the miles in anticipation as we get closer. Mapping software on mobile
devices takes away much of the anxiety of being
lost when a blue dot pinpoints our exact location.
Over time, we develop relationships with friends
who share the joys of youth and laugh with us at
the common ailments of aging.

This is why tragic events, such as times of cri-
sis, a sudden illness, or the death of a close loved
one, are so disorienting. All the reference points
that shaped our identity have shifted; we're left feeling lost, wondering how we will go on.

We constantly search for markers to make
sense of our world. It could be as simple as finding our toothbrush in the same place each morning or as complicated as wondering if a word of
forgiveness will come from someone we have
harmed. Some markers take on different meaning over time, such as a necklace passed from
one generation to another. Some familiar objects
become agents of transformation; charred bricks
salvaged from a burned home are made into a
flower box for the new one.

What is true for individuals is equally valid for
communities and cultures. Every society shapes
the identity of the group by the way its people
organize their space and the way they tell time.
Archaeologists determine much about the values of ancient people by studying the physical
evidence of the location of neighborhoods, archi-
tectural styles, and the quality of everyday items.
Historians note how the development of different means of measuring time brought profound

changes in the way people related to one another and to the natural world.

Celtic Ireland provides a rich example of how Christianity transformed a people in large part by the way they adapted and reimagined understandings of space and time. In order to see this most clearly, we need to go inside the engines that drove this change—namely, the fascinating and surprising world of monastic settlements.

Sacred Space

Visitors to Ireland today often remark that it seems like a magical place. The land itself seems to be alive. This is due, in part, to the year-round moderate climate producing eternally green landscapes. Every turn in the road produces another view of a rugged coastline or sweeping valley. Mists in the morning lend an air of mystery.

Long before Christianity arrived, the Celtic people already had a deep spiritual connection to the land. Natural wells providing life-giving water were understood to be portals to benevolent spirits dwelling deep within. Certain locations along the coast or on elevated spaces seemed to teem with the energy of the spirit world. There they would build mounds of rock or other stone structures to mark them as places for festivals and prayers. This strong tradition of spirituality provided a fertile field for the seeds of Christianity to grow.

As the new religion slowly supplanted the old, it maintained and reinterpreted much of the shape and values of the existing culture. People were accustomed to living in small, independent villages where they were loyally attached to the tribe and the local leader rather than to a distant monarch. Some of the young people would choose to leave to join the one group that transcended all the local clans—the druids. They served religious functions, to be sure, but they provided many more services. They were the teachers, the keepers of the stories of the past, and the dispensers of judgment in certain disputes. When local skirmishes broke out between tribes, they served as referees, stepping in to halt the killing when one side was losing so many men as to threaten sustainable life in the village.

It seemed natural then that Christians would look to congregate in independent communities. It was slow going at first, in part because Patrick and other leaders tried to impose a diocese system on the island. This model, developed on the continent, was dependent on cities to serve as the seat of an area bishop. Since there were no cities in Ireland and the people resisted centralized authority, the effort failed to take root.

The monastic tradition from the Egyptian desert, however, provided a model that fit more neatly with Celtic society. The first monastery in Celtic lands was established by Ninian on the west coast of Scotland in the late fourth century. A few other settlements gained adherents on the Irish mainland until the sixth century, which witnessed a surge in the development of monasteries across the island. This rapid growth was driven by many factors. By this time, the number of Christians reached a critical mass, enough that young people now turned to the church to offer an outlet for their spiritual enthusiasm and to find a sense of purpose. Others sought escape from the anxiety caused by the yellow plague that took the lives of many, young and old. The European continent was slipping into the "Dark Ages" as society disintegrated in the wake of the collapse of the Roman Empire. Literacy rates and religious devotion plummeted as political systems fell into chaos.

The monasteries that developed in the Celtic world were not the stereotypical cloistered communities of monks or nuns following strict rules. These looked more like their familiar villages with a mix of different types of people. Some had males and females, married and celibate, lay and clergy—all in the same community. Some members were ascetics who lived apart from the group for long periods of time to practice their simple, self-denying way of life. Others tilled the land or raised livestock. Some were engaged in acts of hospitality and caring for the poor.

There were certainly similarities among the monasteries, but there was no standard rule that all had to follow. This allowed creative adaptation to the needs of the local area and the personalities of the members. These communities ranged in population from a handful of faithful souls to hundreds and, in rare cases, such as Clonnard, as many as three thousand. Some of the larger monasteries developed satellite communities—the whole collective was called a *parachia*—among which there were kindred bonds but not enforced compliance of a strict code.

The location of these communities was also just as varied; the only common element was that they were near a source of fresh water. Glendalough, for example, was in the forested Wicklow Mountains, Kildare on the rolling plains, and Clonmacnoise by the River Shannon. Some were in remote but accessible locations, and others at the crossroads of heavily traveled transportation routes.

So what would motivate a person in that time to join a monastic community? One popular reason was the desire to pursue religious devotion. Charismatic figures and those renowned for their holiness tended to attract a following. People wanted to be near them to learn from their wisdom. Monasteries offered a rigorous life where a person could focus on developing their faith free from family expectations. Many young people seeking to find their place in the world found opportunities to challenge themselves by willingly taking on the commitments of belonging to a religious order.

In early medieval Ireland, a monastery was a prime location for those wanting to be near the center of the action and to escape a provincial life. In the absence of cities, these communities became gathering places for occasional markets and political conferences. They served as repositories for valuables since there were no banks, and without prisons, some local troublemakers were sent there for the brothers and sisters to keep an eye on them.

Irish monasteries became centers of intellectual, spiritual, and artistic expression. When learning was compromised on the continent, schools in Ireland were flourishing. Many had a building known as a scriptorium, where members made copies of the Bible and other ancient texts. Artisans brought their skills to produce beautiful liturgical objects in service to the church.

The rhythm of life in a monastery is captured beautifully in this prayer ascribed to Saint Columba:

> Let me bless almighty God, whose
>   power extends over sea and land,
>   whose angels watch over all.
>
> Let me study sacred books to calm my
>   soul; I pray for peace, kneeling at
>   heaven's gates.
>
> Let me do my daily work, gathering
>   seaweed, catching fish, giving
>   food to the poor.
>
> Let me say my daily prayers,
>   sometimes chanting, sometimes
>   quiet, always thanking God.
>
> Delightful it is to live on a peaceful isle,
>   in a quiet cell, serving the King of
>   kings. [1]

Thin Places

When I was a child, my parents bought a five-acre plot of land a couple of miles west of town. At the time, it was considered "out in the country." Building a house there was a challenge: There were only dirt roads, no public utilities, and a lot of trees and brush to clear. Dad worked the night shift at his job in Tulsa, and he and Mom worked on the house during the day. They created an idyllic setting for my sister and me to grow up.

Now when I visit as an adult, we travel over paved roads past new housing additions to a place that seems strangely smaller. Even though the house has been remodeled several times over the years, it still feels familiar. Sitting down to dinner in the kitchen brings back memories of the many times we gathered there for meals, each of us in the same seats every time. There are fewer trees now, but many still remain that we hid behind when we hosted the church youth group on Sunday nights for games of "Kick the Can." I sleep peacefully in the same room where my parents comforted me when I was afraid of the dark.

What appears as just another house to most people has become for me sacred ground. That particular site and what happened there connects me to memories, to family, to that which shaped my identity. It is what some Celtic scholars have called a "thin place," where the space between the spirit world and the physical world becomes very narrow, where a sense of the transcendent breaks through.

We all know such places. For some the experience is very personal, such as a church campground where they made a decision to follow Christ or a favorite pew where they sat with a grandparent in worship. Some thin places are more public, such as the 9/11 Memorial in New York City or the natural wonder of the Grand Canyon.

Monasteries in Ireland were often built on sites already recognized as places of particular connection to the spirit world. Paths worn smooth over decades by pilgrims seeking spiritual renewal or help in time of need now led to Christians ready to assist them. The monasteries offered not a withdrawal from the realities of life but an alternate vision of what the world could be every day in every place. They kept alive the flame lit by the Hebrew prophets of a world of justice and peace, what Jesus called the kingdom or the reign of God, and projected that light into the surrounding countryside.

While the monasteries were considered sacred spaces, some areas within the grounds were especially holy. Churches where the community gathered to pray; a structure housing relics of revered people, such as the founder of the monastery; and cemeteries were particular places that straddled the threshold between the spirit world and the physical one. Over the years, these sections were marked with signs indicating their boundaries. None of these markers were more dramatic than the high-standing crosses that developed in the eighth century.

High-Standing Crosses

After several days in the west and north of Ireland, our study-abroad group was approaching Dublin to prepare for our flight home. We had one more stop on the itinerary. Just off the M1 motorway sit the ruins of the once-thriving Christian settlement of Monasterboice. We had already visited several locations that looked very similar, so now, this late in the trip, enthusiasm was running low. Walking along one more rock wall, through another copse of trees, past more tombstones was all routine until we turned the corner. "Now that's a cross," one of our students called out.

What evoked his response was his first look at Muiredach's Cross, the finest example of this art form in the Celtic lands. While most of the hundreds of these sandstone crosses scattered over the island are 10–12 feet tall, this one stands nineteen feet and is twenty inches thick. The sheer bulk of this cross seemed to have a magnetic effect, drawing us close, inviting us to look attentively at the carved depictions of the Crucifixion and the Last Judgment, David and Goliath, and the adoration of the magi.

These crosses, unique to the Celtic world, have their origins in the standing stones from pre-Christian times. Large boulders situated in fields marked the boundaries of grazing areas, while others placed along established pathways served as signposts to travelers. Christians etched cross patterns onto these stones, once more modifying cultural symbols for religious use. In time, they moved on from rock slabs to build free-standing crosses.

The Celts favored a particular design that featured a standard t-shape with a circle set immediately behind or around where the arms of the cross joined. We can only speculate the meaning of this distinctive look. The most practical explanation suggests the lower pieces of the circle were needed to brace the horizontal arms. But the Celts' appreciation of symbols and the quality of their stonemasons cause us to look for more spiritual interpretations. Some have suggested that the circle depicts the wreath given to military heroes in Rome showing Christ's victory over the forces of evil. Others see it as a halo representing the holiness of the one who died there. The circle, without beginning or ending, has long been understood as a symbol of eternal life. I think the best explanation, however, lies in the echoes of pre-Christian times.

The circle was a pagan sign depicting the sun or the earth, the natural world. By superimposing this sign on the cross, the Celts expressed their view that the revelation of God comes to us through the natural world and in the person of Jesus Christ. We need both to get the full picture, so the two are bound together with the circle at the intersection of the natural and the spiritual realms.

The carvings on these crosses range from simple, abstract designs to biblical scenes from both the Hebrew Bible and the New Testament or events from local history. Historians believe that the crosses were originally painted in bright colors, suggesting that they may have functioned much as icons do in the Eastern church. As the members gathered for worship or as individuals approached the cross for a time of personal devotion, gazing at the images opened a window into the spirit world. They did not pray *to* the icon, but *through* the icon, where the stories of the lives of those who had gone before inspired and guided the Christians now taking their place in the line of the faithful.

Sacred Time

Ask someone to tell you the time, and more than likely they will glance at their wristwatch or to a wall clock, maybe look to a computer or cell-phone screen. Their answer will probably be very precise—2:15 or 20 minutes to 5:00. Ancient, tribal people would find this utterly incomprehensible. The same question posed to them would evoke a glance toward the sky or perhaps to the woods to observe the behavior of the animals. They were very much in tune with the rhythms of nature and located themselves in relation to that arena; we impose a set of arbitrary numbers on time that have no relationship to the natural world.

Should we pose the simple question "When does the day begin?" ancient people would offer "sunrise" or "sunset" as logical answers. For modern people, the answer is "midnight," a misnamed point that changes in relation to the movement of the sun, the time of year, and the location from the equator.

Most cultures, however, agree that time is measured in two basic ways: linear and cyclical. Linear time is what we experience moving from point A to point B and beyond. An example would be the progress of human development—from birth to childhood, adolescence, adulthood, and death. Rites of passage denote the movement through these stages. Cyclical time marks events recurring at regular times. The changing seasons, birthdays, and anniversaries illustrate this model.

The Bible has different ways of dealing with time. The Greek word *chronos* refers to time that can be measured and identified, while *kairos* refers to getting lost in the moment, such as spending time with a loved one or being caught up in a spiritual experience, so that you look up and wonder where the time went.

Winston Churchill famously said, "We shape our buildings and afterwards our buildings shape us."[2] The same can be said by the way we organize our time. What we put at the center indicates what we value most; moving through that time increasingly forms us into the image of what we honor. In the Roman world, the year was somewhat connected to the movements of the sun and the moon, but the focus was a series of regular festivals celebrating agricultural seasons and various gods and goddesses. The day was organized around the marketplace: opening, mid-morning, lunch, mid-afternoon, and closing.

The early Christians resisted the pressure to be conformed to Roman values and religion. They made the radical step of changing the calendar so that the year was organized around the story of Jesus. At the center was the celebration of Easter. Over time, Epiphany, Christmas, and Pentecost became distinct seasons with days noting events in the life of Jesus becoming part of the tradition.

To organize the day, they followed the Jewish practice of pausing at certain prescribed times to pray, read from the Psalms, and sing hymns. We see this in the Book of Acts. Peter and John were on their way to the Temple for ninth-hour prayers when they healed a lame man. A few days later, Peter was engaged in sixth-hour prayer on a rooftop in Joppa when he received the vision of a sheet from heaven bearing clean and unclean animals.

Before Christianity arrived, the Celtic calendar was centered on the movements of the natural world. The spring and autumnal equinox and winter and summer solstices divided the year into quadrants. Halfway through each of these sections, other festivals focused on the agricultural cycle. Imbolc[3] on February 1 celebrated the ewes beginning to produce milk for their young. Beltaine on May 1 marked the beginning of summer when the cattle were put out to pasture. Lughnasa on August 1 was a grand harvest festival.

But the most important holiday was Samhain on October 31. This marked the transition from summer to winter, from light to darkness, and was considered their New Year's Day. Earlier we discussed how certain locations were regarded as thin places, where the spirit world and the physical world came very close together. Samhain was the equivalent in time; they believed the thin membrane separating the two worlds actually opened on this night, allowing spirits to revisit their old home places. This was welcomed by some as an opportunity to cherish memories of loved ones who had passed. But the open door didn't discriminate on who came through, so some people were struck with fear that they would be visited by an old enemy who might wish them harm. They started putting on masks to trick the malevolent spirits from recognizing them. We continue a playful interpretation of this holiday today on Halloween.

So for hundreds of years, Celtic society had been shaped by the movements of nature and the land. They adapted quite easily to the Christian practice of the liturgical year, in part because they reinterpreted their existing festivals with new meaning. Beltaine, for example, always included a large bonfire. This holiday occurred around the same time as Easter, so it was a short step to reinterpret this as the paschal fire lit for the vigil service. And while Christians didn't believe that the spirits of dead persons reappeared on October 31, they did honor all those faithful who had gone before. Thus All Saints Day on November 1 became the occasion to remember their example.

The daily regimen of prayer, however, really caught the imagination of the Celtic Christians. The continental Christians had already adapted the Jewish model so that their prayer times coincided with the Roman market timetable while adding prayers at dawn and bedtime. The rigorous Celts took this one step further, adding an eighth prayer time in the middle of the night.

There is a revival of interest in observing the Christian Year and in practicing fixed-hour prayer. An increasing number of people are reclaiming the wisdom of the early church in making Christ the center around which everything else revolves. When we hear about praying at regular times, we most readily think of Muslims who have been much more faithful in practicing this particular spiritual exercise common to many religions.

A friend of mine related an experience she had while shopping in a Turkish bazaar in Istanbul. She found a rug she wanted to buy, and as is the custom, she started negotiating with the shopkeeper on the price. Just when she thought they were about to close the deal, he left—just walked away. She was confused and a little bit offended. After a few minutes he returned, picked up where they left off, and sold the rug. It was only later when reflecting on this encounter that she realized what happened. She remembered hearing the call to prayer go out just before he disappeared. There was nothing more important for that man at that moment than to pray. He was taking a chance that his eager customer would be gone when he got back, but it didn't matter. It was time to pray.

It would be easy to dismiss such faithfulness to this practice as empty ritual or even legalistic conformity. But fixed-hour prayer taps into something much more profound. Prayer at certain times throughout the day not only renders those moments sacred but every moment in between as well. It makes a radical statement that our faith forms the center around which our day revolves, not mealtimes, not work or school schedules, not to-do lists. While regular prayer may be adapted into these routines, those recurring moments of pausing in deference to our faith constantly remind us of what is most important.

Because we're so accustomed to viewing time as something that we manage, it's difficult to view it sacramentally, as a gift from God with opportunities of grace. Theologian Dorothy Bass notes that in the hymn of Creation that opens the Bible, after each creative act—calling forth light, sky, waters—God sees the goodness of what has been made, and the narrator declares, "And there was evening and there was morning, the first (second, third, fourth, fifth, sixth) day . . ."[4] To our ears, it sounds as if the narrator got it backwards—shouldn't it be morning, then evening?

Eugene Peterson, pastor and author, believes that the Hebrew writers got it right from a theological perspective. While we tend to think that the day begins at sunrise, the Jews believe that the day begins at sunset. That's why the Sabbath begins on Friday night. It seems rather odd that the day would begin while we are sleeping, but that's just the point. The first part of the day passes in darkness but not in inactivity. God is at work, growing the crops, knitting together the wound, preparing the way. When we wake, we join in the work that God is already doing.[5] We don't start the day or even seize the day; we receive the day as a gift. Time is not ours to possess or control: It belongs to God, who invites us to participate as trustees of this most precious offering.

At the same time the high-standing crosses were being built in Celtic lands, round towers were also rising into the sky. These stone structures, ranging 60–130 feet tall, served as Christian minarets. At the appointed time, a member of the community climbed the steps to ring a bell calling the people to prayer. Their great height allowed the sound to travel a greater distance so that all in the area—whether they were plowing a field, washing dishes, or maybe even selling a rug—would know it was time to honor the Lord of time.

It was not just about regular prayer for the Celtic Christians; the specific time was important as well. They believed that the hosts of heaven followed a prayer schedule of their own, and it was incumbent upon those on earth to get in sync with this pattern. While that may sound a little strange to us, the theological truth behind it is instructive. Prayer is not trying to convince God to come into line with our desires; it is to bring ourselves into harmony with what God is already doing. This is expressed in one of the most familiar Celtic prayers known as Saint Patrick's Breastplate in its famous stanza:

> Christ with me, Christ before me, Christ behind me,

Christ in me, Christ beneath me, Christ
above me,
Christ on my right, Christ on my left,
Christ when I lie down, Christ when I sit
down, Christ when I rise,
Christ in the heart of every man who
thinks of me,
Christ in the mouth of every one who
speaks of me,
Christ in every eye that sees me,
Christ in every ear that hears me.[6]

Aligning Coordinates

After our study-abroad group left Newgrange
Tomb, our Irish guide, Pat, announced that he
had arranged for us to visit a smaller passage
grave known as Four Knocks. He explained that
it wouldn't be quite as dramatic as the one we
just experienced, but it would be a more personal
encounter. In fact, our group would be the only
people there.

We soon discovered why. After meandering
along country roads in the middle of nowhere,
we pulled up in front of a metal gate with a large
padlock guarding a cow pasture. Pat was hoping
it would be unlocked but was soon disappointed.
When he had called about gaining entrance, he
was given vague directions to a house where he
could get the key. As we drove trying to find it, Pat
and the driver both looked very uncertain, even
after we saw a sign posted by the Office of Public
Works that made sense only if you were already
familiar with the area:

Key Available from
Mr. Fintan White
Turn LEFT at Cross
5th House on Right
(Kilmoon Rd.) 1 Mile

After a few minutes, we saw a man walking along the dirt road. The driver stopped, and Pat leaned out the door, "Do you know where Mr. Fintan White lives?" The man pointed in the direction we were already going and acknowledged our thanks with a nod of his head. We soon came to a modest house with children's toys scattered in the front yard. A woman answered the door and explained to Pat that Mr. White was not currently at home but was expected any moment. It wasn't long before the man we met on the road approached, walked past the bus, and proceeded directly into the house. Mr. Fintan White himself!

I've often wondered why Mr. White didn't identify himself on the road and allow us to give him a ride the rest of the way. I've come to believe that the answer lies in the land—the ancient passage tombs, the holy wells, the standing crosses, the call to prayer reverberating over the hills and through the hearts of the faithful. We weren't the first group of wide-eyed tourists he had encountered, and we wouldn't be the last. Mr. White had become one with the steady, healing rhythm of life.

The spiritual markers honed through years of patient practice guide us in times of confusion; remind us how far we have come; and always, always point us to the one who makes all things new.

4

Hospitality on the Journey

I f you're planning a road trip in Ireland for the first time, I do not advise planning your itinerary using Google Maps from the comfort of your living room. I speak from experience. A few years ago, our family spent a couple of days in Dublin, then rented a car to see the country. Before leaving the United States, I had anticipated where we would be each evening and booked lodging in bed and breakfasts for each stop. I learned very quickly that driving times in Ireland are much different from those in the United States. Most roads in Ireland are two-lane and go through every small village along the way. The beauty and charm are unmatched but not easy to appreciate if you expect to get on down the road.

We woke up the third morning in Donegal Town in the northwest corner of the island. Our reservations for that night were at a cozy inn housed in a converted eighteenth-century linen mill. It was in the countryside just outside Downpatrick near the northeast coast only 175 miles away. Plenty of time to do a little sightseeing along the way—or so we thought. After a short detour to see Grianan Ailligh, a stone ring fort over two thousand years old, we ate lunch in Derry and toured the Bogside neighborhood, site of so much tension during the Troubles of the twentieth century. Then it was off to the Giant's Causeway, a collection of dramatic geological formations on the north coast. We arrived there too late to take the trams to the park, so we walked over a mile each way to enjoy the stunning natural beauty jutting out into the sea. By now darkness was approaching, and we still had eighty-five miles to go!

So on narrow roads, in a relentless rain, tired and hungry, we pushed on. The British woman on the GPS was trying her best to help us find our way, but we still missed a few turns. When we passed a beautiful, flood-lit building in Belfast,[1] I said, "Take a good look, kids. We'll figure out what that is later." Finally, we made it into the countryside past Downpatrick and realized that we were completely lost. We stopped and called Aidan, the owner of the inn. "What do you see around you?" he asked. We didn't see much, but it was enough for him to know where we were. "Don't move. I'll be there in five minutes." As promised, he soon pulled alongside, and we followed him through several turns, then over a cattle gate onto a rutted path through a field, when suddenly this beautiful inn seemed to appear out of nowhere.

Aidan and his wife, Theresa, received us warmly and showed us to our room. It was past 9:00 P.M., and we were wet, miserable, and starving. We asked if there was a place in town where we could hear some live music and get something to eat. "No, there's no music this late on a week-night, and I think the restaurants are closed. There may be a Chinese place open." We were in no mood to get back out in the rain for Asian food in Northern Ireland, so we said we would eat some snacks we brought with us.

"Would you like some homemade bread?" Aidan asked. "Sure." Theresa started stirring around in the kitchen. "How about some cheese and deli meat?" "Okay." "I'll make some hot chocolate for the kids." Soon we were sitting at the counter with a makeshift feast spreading before us. When they learned about the miles we had covered that day, their reaction confirmed that we had obviously attempted a route any local person would imme-diately deem crazy. "I think you need a Guinness," Theresa whispered to Ann. After a few minutes of easy conversation, a warm hearth, and the sound of gentle rain, the tension drained away, our shoul-ders relaxed, and we settled in for a night of peace-ful sleep.

Many ancient cultures ranked hospitality to strangers and guests as a primary virtue; the Celts were no exception. If a member of the community refused to open their door to visitors, they would be shamed and even shunned by the rest of the village. Every Irish monastery had a guesthouse, usually situated in a prime location on the grounds. Being away from home left the traveler vulnerable; to refuse hospitality could leave them susceptible to hunger, foul play, or even death.

As our family discovered that chilly October evening, the simplest words or actions can bring a sense of stability and comfort to those who have lost their way. "You are welcome here" transports us from darkness to light, fear to safety, alienation to inclusion. "You are welcome here" creates a space where new relationships are formed and strangers become friends. "You are welcome here" restores hope and confidence and enables us to continue the journey.

This is true whether we are traveling physical highways or traversing the seasons of the spirit. If we walk the path of faith long enough, we will go through deserts of doubt and disappointment. We will cry out with the psalmist and with Jesus when feeling forsaken by God. We will wonder if we're on the right road at all. That is when we need the embrace of community, if not to answer all the questions, then at least to offer a haven in the midst of the storm.

Pastoral theologian Robert Dykstra relates the story of Edmund Steimle, noted Lutheran preacher and homiletics professor. Steimle's wife of many years, Rosalind, died on a Saturday before Easter:

> She got sick suddenly in the morning, sicker in the afternoon, and by nightfall she was gone. Steimle said, "I found myself the next day seated in the pew of my church on Easter Sunday, a church full of Easter lilies and a brass choir and a springtime congregation singing the 'Alleluia's,' and they stuck in my throat. I couldn't sing them, I did not believe in the resurrection, not that day, not with what had happened to me. I put down the hymn book. But as

I listened to the congregation sing,
I realized, "I don't have to believe in the
resurrection today. They are believing
in the resurrection for me until I can
believe in it again for myself."[2]

Offering hospitality to others has long been regarded as a spiritual discipline. Welcoming strangers is deeply embedded in Scripture and is referenced by Jesus as one of the signs of his true disciples (Matthew 25:31-46). Stories abound in the Celtic Christian tradition of hospitality shown to other people as well as to animals. This comes to fullest expression in Ireland in the person of Saint Brigid of Kildare.

Stories of the Saints

The history of Celtic Christianity is populated with a number of individuals referred to as "saints," not due to a formal canonization process but because people of the region saw them as possessing particular spiritual depth and devotion, worthy of imitation.

From the earliest days of the church, the lives of special persons were celebrated in stories told for generations. The collection of these accounts, known as hagiographies ("writings of the saints"), often stylized the stories to illustrate certain characteristics of the person. The authors were concerned not so much with literal truth as with spiritual truth to inspire the readers to more godly living.

The Celts already had a long history of legendary tales explaining how they came to Ireland by defeating a race of demigods and stories of mythic heroes such as Queen Maeve and the mighty warrior Cuchulain. The practice of writing hagiographies proved too wonderful to resist, and when they took up the pen, they put their own spin on the tradition, as they did so many other aspects of Christianity. They read more like folklore with the saints controlling the weather, interacting with animals, performing miracles of healing, and possessing insight into people's innermost thoughts. They are intended to be highly entertaining while always pointing toward deeper spiritual truths.

Saint Brigid

The saints regarded as the most significant among the Celts are Patrick (390–461), Brigid (452–524), and Columba (521–597). Some may be surprised to see a woman in this list, but not those familiar with the social structure of pre-Christian Ireland. Women had more standing and rights in Celtic society than in other cultures of the time. They could divorce their husbands for several causes, including infidelity and spousal abuse. At the time of marriage, their dowry was held in trust so that at the time of divorce, the woman would take back her dowry plus half of any wealth attained during the marriage. There are also stories of women engaging in battle, most famously Queen Boudica, who led her tribe against the Romans in first-century southern England. So we would expect to include women among those who shaped the direction and emphases of this new religion in an extraordinary land.

Brigid established her base in Kildare, on the plains of eastern Ireland, where she founded a monastery that housed both men and women. From there she often traveled around the island establishing other religious communities, building a network that became one of the strongest in Ireland. Although Brigid probably never met Patrick, that didn't stop the hagiographers from telling stories that showed her superiority to the great man, even falling asleep during one of his sermons!

Her real strength, however, was not her administrative skills but her commitment to live out the gospel in sharing the love of Christ and in practicing radical hospitality. The stories of her heroic acts echo biblical narratives, especially from the life and ministry of Jesus.

This is evident beginning in the story of her birth. Her mother, Broicsech, a Christian slave woman, became pregnant by her owner, Dubthach, a pagan Leinster noble. In shades of Abraham, Sarah, and Hagar, his wife demanded that he send the slave woman away. He sold her to a kindly druid but retained the rights to the unborn child.

One day, Broicsech suddenly went into labor as she approached the house on her way back from milking the cows. She gave birth on the threshold of the house and immediately washed the baby in the fresh milk as a symbol of new life and purity. This story also signifies how the Celtic Christians saw Brigid as a transition figure—between paganism and the new faith, between sexism and equality, between material and spiritual wealth.[3] Her ministry would be one of crossing boundaries and redefining what it meant to live in community now guided by the light of Christ.

True to his word, Brigid's father returned to reclaim his daughter, a decision he soon regretted. Blind to her special gifts, he assigned her to menial tasks such as herding animals, churning butter, and cooking. With such free access to the food, Brigid had other ideas about what to do with it. Any hungry person or dog passing by was treated to a feast. Her father grew so annoyed at Brigid that he loaded her in his chariot and drove to the royal fort to sell her into slavery. "Whatever she lays her hand on, she takes," Dubthach complained to the king. While it was not yet apparent, the father had already made another mistake; he left Brigid alone in the chariot when he went inside. While the negotiations were in process, a beggar walked by and asked for assistance. Looking around, Brigid saw her father's ceremonial sword, which she promptly handed over to the starving man with instructions to sell it and buy some food. This really pushed Dubthach over the edge, but Brigid was undeterred: "I gave it to Christ." The king, either because he was more insightful or merely to protect his own possessions, released Brigid to pursue whatever life she chose.[4]

For Brigid, that meant making a commitment to a life of celibacy devoted to God. At the ceremony when the sisters took the veil, each was to identify her favorite beatitude. Unsurprisingly, Brigid chose, "Blessed are the merciful," the characteristic that motivated her life and actions from childhood. As she read the Gospels, she listened as Jesus said that caring for the least of these—the hungry, the poor, those in prison—was caring for Christ himself. She watched as Jesus practiced a radical hospitality that welcomed all people without regard for their station in life. She thought nothing of the reckless generosity of the shepherd leaving 99 sheep in the fold in order to search for the one who was lost. And she lived out the example of Jesus time after time.

> One day when Brigid was on a long journey, she stopped to rest by the wayside. A wealthy lady, on hearing that Brigid was in the neighborhood, brought her a beautiful basket of choice apples. No sooner had the gift been presented than a group of poor people came by and begged for food. Without hesitation Brigid distributed to them the choice apples. The donor was utterly disgusted and said to Brigid, "I brought those apples for you, not for them." And Brigid's reply was "What is mine is theirs."[5]

I find the attitude of the donor particularly interesting. Apparently the intention behind her gift was to gain favor with Brigid, perhaps to win a blessing from the great woman. She was living out of a theology of scarcity, the belief that there is a finite amount of goods and services and we need to work every angle to make sure we get preferential treatment, even if it means that others go without. Brigid, on the other hand, was working out of a theology of abundance, the belief that the blessings of God know no limit. We give, not for what we might receive in return, but in imitation of the one who showed us that giving is the way to life.

Other stories made more explicit parallels between Brigid and the life of Jesus. For instance, she once turned water into milk to ease the pain of a young woman who had fallen ill, and on another occasion she turned water into beer to the delight of a group of thirsty lepers. This is an obvious reference to Jesus turning water into wine at a wedding in Cana of Galilee. While it may appear that the point of these stories is to demonstrate miraculous power, the deeper meaning brings us back to offering hospitality to those in need.

While Jesus is enjoying the wedding, it seems that despite the best efforts of the hosts, the preparations are not enough: They run out of wine. Perhaps more people than they were expecting showed up, or there was a mistake with the guest list; whatever the reason, they come up short. When pressed by his mother to help, Jesus orders the water pots to be filled to the brim. After the servants comply, the wedding planner dips in a ladle only to draw out wine, and not the cheap stuff—the best vintage. Notice that these water pots hold twenty or thirty gallons each—and there were six of them! So let's do the math: Six times twenty, six times thirty—120–180 gallons of wine!

This is obviously more than such a gathering could possibly drink, if we're talking about wine. But if we're talking about the love of God, we see that Jesus brings that in abundance. Instead of getting stingy and fighting over what little is left, Jesus opens the tap of God's extravagant grace, an outpouring of mercy.

I had the privilege of serving as an associate pastor at Boston Avenue United Methodist Church in Tulsa for six years. This dynamic congregation is housed in a beautiful art deco building with a sanctuary that seats 1,300 people in an intimate, sacred setting. At the front of this stunning room is a hand-carved wooden altar rail that elegantly curves across the length of the chancel. When serving Communion, each minister would be assigned a particular section of the rail. As people knelt, we offered them the paten of wafers with one hand and the tray of little juice cups with the other. On one particular Sunday morning, most everyone had been served when I noticed three little girls come toward the front. Their movements were awkward; I don't know why no adult was with them, but it soon became obvious that this was their first time to participate in a Communion service. They held back for a moment, then all three of them practically ran and knelt directly in front of me. I put the trays before them, but instead of reaching for the elements, they just stared at them. Finally, the oldest of the girls looked up at me and asked, "How much do we get?" "One of each," I replied. "You may have one of each." That was the correct answer, practically speaking, but the more truthful response would have been, "Take as much as you want. This is the grace of God, and there is always more than enough!"

A prayer attributed to Saint Brigid captures the inclusive welcome and theology of abundance offered to all:

> I should like a great lake of finest ale for
> the King of kings.

I should like a table of the choicest
food for the family of heaven.
Let the ale be made from the fruits of
faith, and the food be forgiving
love.
I should welcome the poor to my feast,
for they are God's children.
I should welcome the sick to my feast,
for they are God's joy.
Let the poor sit with Jesus at the
highest place, and the sick dance
with the angels.
God bless the poor, God bless the sick,
and bless our human race.
God bless our food, God bless our
drink.
All homes, O God, embrace.[6]

A Life of Hospitality

Several months ago, one of my colleagues
came into my office to ask if I had heard of Lorenza
Andrade Smith. I had not, but I soon learned that
she is a United Methodist clergyperson from San
Antonio. A couple of years previously, she asked to
be appointed to a ministry of presence and advo-
cacy with the homeless. She sold her car and most
of her possessions, took a vow of poverty, and
began living on the streets. Her bishop requires her
to carry an iPhone for safety and to share her ministry through Facebook and e-mail. Lorenza agrees
to accept invitations to travel but no honoraria. She
insists on sleeping on the streets or in shelters.
    Our university hosted her one September as part
of Homeless Awareness Week. One afternoon, we

agreed to meet at a nearby McDonald's. I arrived
at the appointed time and didn't see her, so I went
inside and searched the restaurant. Still no Lorenza.
I called her cell phone and learned that she was
in the parking lot on the other side. She had been
at the bus stop visiting with the people waiting
there. As we drove to our next function, she told
me about the woman suffering terrible illnesses,
the man having trouble finding work—people I had
driven by every day and never noticed.

As we got better acquainted, I learned that this
is her way of life. She gravitates to those overlooked, and even stigmatized, by the larger society. She's been arrested for nonviolent protests
of unjust laws, even going on sustained fasts in
solidarity with the hungry. Everywhere she goes,
she carries a simple metal chalice and paten as a
symbol of her devotion to Christ and the motivation
for her ministry. The more I was around this unas-
suming woman, short of stature but mighty in faith,
the more I realized that I was in the presence of a
modern-day Brigid. They would be very much at
home in each other's presence.

Henri Nouwen wrote,

> Hospitality . . . means primarily
> the creation of a free space where the
> stranger can enter and become a friend
> instead of an enemy. Hospitality is not
> to change people, but to offer them
> space where change can take place.
> It is not to bring men and women over
> to our side, but to offer freedom not dis-
> turbed by dividing lines. It is not to lead

our neighbor into a corner where there are no alternatives left, but to open a wide spectrum of options for choice and commitment.[7]

Very few of us can make the type of commitment people such as Brigid and Lorenza have taken, but we all can be inspired by their example. We can be more intentional about noticing the forgotten ones and doing more to be their advocates. We can consider the needs of others and not focus exclusively on what's best for ourselves. At times, we may be called to go against the status quo through public action that may be way out of our comfort zone. But let's not neglect the countless opportunities we have each day to be a welcoming presence to those in need, perhaps even those closest to us.

In seminary, I worked part-time on campus for the theological journal published there. One afternoon, I came into work upset about something. Nancy, the office manager, and I had had many conversations, so I felt comfortable venting my problems to her. After a few minutes, I moved on and took up a task in an adjoining room. The editor of the journal, one of my professors, Craig Dykstra, came in to work on a few things. I heard Nancy in her not-so-soft whisper say to him, "You better go check on Rod. He's really mad." The next instant, Dr. Dykstra walked in the door. He pulled a chair directly across from me, took off his sport jacket, draped it over the back of the chair, sat down, and asked, "What's going on?" I don't remember any details after that. There's no need.

In just a few seconds, with his simple actions, he let me know that there was nothing more important for him to do right then than to be present for me—that I mattered. He created a "space where change can take place."

Four days after our son, Carus, started the eighth grade, I attended the open house at his middle school. By that time, there was not much to discuss with the teachers, but we went around to each class to chat and to get a sense of what the year had in store. Before walking into his language arts classroom, he whispered to me, "This teacher is cool." When I introduced myself as Carus's father, her face lit up: "Oh, you're the one." Parents are never sure what to expect after that kind of greeting. What was she getting ready to tell me? "We have a new student in our class this year, a little Muslim boy," she told me. "Some of the kids were asking him about his religion. He was having a hard time explaining in a way they could understand, and some of them were starting to get a little aggressive in their questions, making for an uncomfortable situation. Your son spoke up in his defense, gave a few basic facts about Islam, and let them know that there was nothing to fear." Then with a twinkle in her eye she said to me, "I wonder where he got that from?"

I simply said, "Thank you. We're very proud of him," but what I wanted to say was, "Abraham, and Jesus, and the people at his church, and the teachers who encouraged him when he was down, and everyone who saw him as a person of worth regardless of his behavior or attitude or what he could contribute."

On our spiritual journeys, we all need times of refreshment, to be encouraged, to be loved unconditionally. The blessing we seek is usually not found in actively pursuing it; it comes as a result of offering that very gift to others, as stated beautifully in this Celtic rune of hospitality:

> I saw a stranger yesterday;
> I put food in the eating place,
> drink in the drinking place,
> music in the listening place;
> and in the sacred name of the Triune
>   God
> he blessed myself and my house,
> my cattle and my dear ones,
> and the lark said in her song:
> often, often, often,
> goes the Christ in the stranger's guise.[8]

At Home in the World

As with most tribal cultures, the Celts understood their relationship with the natural world as a spiritual connection. In the modern world, we tend to have an objective view of nature as something outside ourselves. The scientific method only reinforces this notion; nature is to be probed, studied, and controlled. Recent developments have caused us to see the interconnectedness of all creation, but we are still discerning what that means theologically. The Celts understood this intuitively and offer helpful insights as we journey toward greater awareness of the relationship between the spiritual and the physical worlds.

Casual readers of early Celtic sources sometimes accuse these people of ascribing to pantheism—the belief that God is everything (*pan* = all, *theism* = God). God doesn't exist outside of the natural world. But a closer reading reveals a more nuanced view. They held instead to a belief known as pan*en*theism—that God is *in* everything. They certainly held the orthodox Christian view that God is separate from the universe (as reflected in Genesis 1) while also being intimately involved and concerned with the world (Genesis 2). To put it another way, the Celts understood the physical world as an expression of God—breathing God's very essence into the physical world just as depicted in the creation of the first human being, who became a living soul only after receiving the divine breath.

All of creation, then, must be given the utmost respect, or as Ninian's Catechism put it, "To perceive the eternal Word of God reflected in every plant and insect, every bird and animal, and every man and woman."

This is behind the many stories in the hagiographies of saints interacting respectfully with animals. According to one account, Cuthbert was walking along a river on a pastoral journey accompanied by a young boy, his traveling companion. As lunch time approached, the youth began to worry that they would find no one along the way who would offer them a meal. About that time, they looked up and saw an eagle flying overhead. Cuthbert said, "This is the eagle that God instructed to provide our lunch." When the eagle lighted by the river, the boy ran over and found a large fish. In his joy, he scooped it up and hurriedly delivered it to Cuthbert.

"What about our fisherman? Why didn't you give him part of it?" the saint asked. Realizing the lesson, the boy took half of the fish back to the eagle before broiling the remainder and sharing it with other men they encountered on the way—enough for all.

In the Celtic world, perhaps no person is regarded as more saintly than Kevin of Glendalough. He retreated to the mountains to find solitude, but his great humility and spiritual depth drew others to him so that a monastic community was formed. Kevin's customary posture to pray was sitting on the floor with his hands outstretched. One day a blackbird lighted in the palm of his hand and laid her eggs there. Because of his tender heart, he remained in that position for days until the tiny birds emerged and took flight.

Paul's Letter to the Romans reflects a similar connection between humanity and the created order. In a particularly moving passage, he tells these Christians how God's love has elevated our lowly standing and made us joint-heirs with Christ, even as we wait for the full realization of that promise. "The whole creation has been groaning in labor pains," Paul writes. "The creation waits with eager longing for the revealing of the children of God" (Romans 8:18-25). The suffering we currently experience because of sin and falling short of God's intentions affects the created order as well. The long-awaited restoration of wholeness is not for us alone, but for the whole of creation.

Perhaps the Christian understanding of nature is seen most profoundly in Jesus as the incarnation of God in human flesh. God honors the natural world that God has made by becoming part of it. As the Gospel of John puts it, God "pitched his tent" among us as one of us. The incarnation speaks volumes of what God thinks about the natural world, to the point of sanctifying it with his very being.

Just showing up would have been a compelling witness, but Jesus went further. At the Crucifixion, God entered most deeply into the human condition by taking our brokenness and the brokenness of the whole created order on himself.

An eleventh-century Celtic poet wrote that in Jesus, God entered our earth community, sharing our flesh, and, in the Resurrection, completed the redemptive act: "Every material and every element and every nature which is seen in the world were all combined in the body in which Christ arose, that is the body of every human person. . . . All the world arose with him, for the nature of all the elements was in the body which Jesus assumed."[9]

In John's telling of the Resurrection story, Mary lingers outside the empty tomb weeping. Even though Jesus stands before her, she mistakes him for the gardener. This garden setting reminds us of the first garden of Creation, when God came looking for Adam and Eve, seeking to establish a relationship, calling their names, only to find them hiding, alienated by their disobedience. Now Jesus stands in a garden, and this time when he calls Mary's name, the relationship is restored.

Too often we tend to divide body and spirit, which God has beautifully created as a whole. Physical bodies are objectified and denigrated as the source of evil. This has led to people abusing the bodies of others and some mistreating their own bodies. Some live with shame because they sense they don't measure up to an arbitrary standard of beauty. Instead of regarding the body as a gateway to greater spiritual life, it is seen as a hindrance to be overcome. I wonder how many lives could be made whole if we returned to the harmonious relationship between body and spirit?

In her novel *Beloved*, Toni Morrison tells the story of newly freed slaves in Ohio coming to grips with what it means to live in this new world while still haunted by the ghosts of the past. For centuries, the bodies of their people had been abused, owned as property, and treated as expendable commodities. In order to move forward, they will have to reclaim their bodies as sacred. They are no longer merely means to a practical end; they are beautiful creations through which they can experience divine love. But all the years of denial and exploitation will not be overcome easily. They need to revive the vision of body and soul reconnected, experienced in their very beings. One prominent character in the novel is an old woman known as Baby Suggs, an unofficial spiritual leader of the community, who calls her flock together in the cathedral of nature:

> When warm weather came, Baby
> Suggs, holy, followed by every black
> man, woman and child who could
> make it through, took her great heart
> to the Clearing—a wide-open place cut
> deep in the woods. . . .

After situating herself on a huge flat-sided rock, Baby Suggs bowed her head and prayed silently. The company watched her from the trees. They knew she was ready when she put her stick down. Then she shouted, "Let the children come!" and they ran from the trees toward her. . . .

"Here," she said, "in this here place, we are flesh; flesh that weeps, laughs; flesh that dances on bare feet in grass. Love it. Love it hard. Yonder they do not love your flesh. They despise it. . . . Love your hands! Love them. Raise them up and kiss them. Touch others with them, pat them together, stroke them on your face 'cause they don't love that either. *You* got to love it, *you!* . . . This is flesh I'm talking about here. Flesh that needs to be loved. . . . Love it, love it, and the beat and beating heart, love that too. . . .

Saying no more, she stood up then and danced with her twisted hip the rest of what her heart had to say while the others opened their mouths and gave her the music.[10]

Jesus performed the ultimate act of hospitality by dwelling among us. He bore in his body our suffering and our joy and now invites us to join in the chorus the morning stars sing together—the praises of the one who has created, and is creating, in love.

5

Reluctant Journeys

My father is one of the most intelligent persons I know. Due to unfortunate family circumstances, he was not able to receive much in the way of formal education, but that didn't stifle his desire to learn. As a young man, he hung around the local garage where the mechanics allowed him to watch them work and ask questions. He was hired on to construction sites where he quickly grasped carpentry skills to the point that he became a master cabinet builder. When my sister and I came along, he sought more stable employment and joined the maintenance crew at a company in Tulsa that built off-shore drilling rigs.

He was particularly proficient in creating solutions to problems that couldn't be solved with standard equipment. Shop supervisors would call on Dad, who would assess the situation, sketch a design, and build what was needed. It was hard work, but he was good at it and found satisfaction in his job.

Because of the volatile nature of the oil business, there were always rumors of the company laying off employees, but they always seemed to keep going. Then the dreaded day of reckoning came: The company filed for bankruptcy and closed the shop.

Dad suddenly was unemployed. At fifty-five years of age and job experience only as a skilled laborer, he didn't fit the profile most hiring managers desired. Despite his best efforts, no call came. Days turned into weeks and weeks into months, the silence slowly taking its toll on his spirit, his sense of identity, and his desire to contribute. To this day, he still speaks of that time as a dark night of the soul, a sojourn in the wilderness where, for the first time in his life, hopelessness began to set in.

One day the phone rang. It was one of his colleagues from his previous place of employment. This friend had found a job working in maintenance for an aeronautics manufacturing company. They were looking for another staff person, and he knew just who they needed. Dad got the job and was immediately impressed by the positive attitude that pervaded the company. He was treated as an honored employee, given even more of those tough problems to solve, and received better benefits on top of that. Those last years before retirement were some of the best of his working life.

All of us face journeys we would rather not take. Some result from poor decisions either we or others have made; some are the result of forces beyond our control. These journeys start in a number of different ways: an unwelcome diagnosis, the effects of aging, adjusting to an empty nest, the breakup of a relationship. Some involve larger social forces at work: small towns struggling as more people move to urban areas, churches experiencing declining membership, racism tearing at the fabric of communities, war creating refugees searching for anyplace to survive.

The Celtic Christians constantly encountered reluctant journeys. Living in a harsh environment, periods of political instability, floods, famine threatening their crops—all these things tested their faith and challenged their resolve to persevere through hardships. One person from this time, however, endured many and varied obstacles to his ministry out of proportion to all others. In spite of, or perhaps because of, his difficult journey, this person happens to be the most famous of all the Celtic saints, the one we know today as Saint Patrick.

Saint Patrick of Ireland

March 17 has become a celebration of all things Irish, especially in the United States. People wear green clothing, and images of shamrocks appear on windows and cupcakes. A number of cities hold parades, most notably New York, Boston, and Savannah, where the many Americans of Irish descent reclaim their heritage, often with bagpipes providing the soundtrack. It's known as Saint Patrick's Day in honor of the date of his death around 1,500 years ago.

What would come as a surprise to many revelers is that the person they honor with this grand celebration was not Irish. If asked to tell the story of Patrick, most would mention how he drove the snakes out of Ireland and taught the doctrine of the

Trinity to the locals by using the three leaves of the shamrock, neither of which is true. The caricature of the man, unfortunately, masks the much more compelling story of one of the most fascinating figures in Christian history.

Much of what we know of Patrick's life comes from two documents he wrote toward the end of his life. In one, known as *Saint Patrick's Confession*, he defends his ministry in Ireland by recounting key events in his life and revealing the motivations behind his decisions. The other is a *Letter to the Soldiers of Coroticus*, in which he vehemently denounces the actions of a British warlord who kidnapped or killed a number of recent Irish converts to Christianity. We also have a few other documents about this man, including two hagiographies, which were written at least two hundred years after his death. As in the case of Brigid, these stories provide more theological than historical information but are insightful into the continuing influence of these honored persons.

Patrick was born around the year 390, probably on the west coast of Britain, to what we would call a middle-class family. His father and grandfather held leadership positions in the local church. All this indicates that the family was well-connected within Roman society as it developed on the edges of the empire. But Patrick's birth came at a time when Rome was pulling its military forces back to the homeland to protect against barbarian invaders. This left a power vacuum making the settled, comfortable society in the region more volatile.

Irish bandits took advantage of this breech in the British defenses. Small groups raided coastal settlements looking for livestock, precious metals, and, especially, able-bodied human beings to be sold into slavery. Such was the fate of Patrick, who at sixteen years of age was kidnapped, taken by force to Ireland, and apparently consigned to a life of servitude.

Tending sheep in the rain and cold, day after day, allowed the young Patrick to reflect upon his life. He admits that he had not been a faithful Christian, but now the Bible stories and spiritual practices of his childhood took on new meaning. He prayed "a hundred times" during the day and again at night, finding comfort in his time of need.

After six years of this monotonous existence, one night while sleeping he heard a voice telling him that his ship was ready and he was going home. This must have confused the young man. In those days, travel in Ireland was extremely dangerous. Following the coastline took a person through the mountains with the challenges of rough terrain, wild animals, and thieves. Moving inland meant negotiating peat bogs and exposure to the elements. No one dared travel alone unless they were a fugitive from justice or a runaway slave. To make matters worse, Patrick had ended up in the northern part of the island, two hundred miles from the closest port. Somehow, he made it to a ship sailing to Britain where his exuberant family welcomed him home, begging him never to leave them again.

But Patrick's rekindled faith compelled him to train for the priesthood, which he did successfully, eventually being made a bishop. Then another visitation in the night would change the course of his life. Much like the apostle Paul's vision of a

Macedonian man saying, "Come over and help us" (Acts 16:6-10). Patrick saw an Irishman who called to him, "Holy boy, we beg you, come back and walk among us again."[1]

Leaving the security of home and the established church to serve in Ireland was by no means a popular choice. His fellow bishops thought he was crazy for even considering going to a land outside "civilization" to a people they regarded almost as subhuman and unworthy of hearing the gospel. It was a sure career killer. Patrick did not make the choice quickly. After the initial visitation, he continued to struggle in prayer, seeking reassurance that this was indeed the call of God on his life.

According to tradition, Patrick returned to Ireland in the year 432 to find scattered communities of Christians, primarily in the south. He seems to have focused his ministry in the north, probably to make inroads among the powerful Uí Néill clan. Motivated by evangelistic zeal, he traveled widely preaching the gospel, baptizing converts, and establishing churches. Success did not come easily or without criticism. He faced abuse from unbelievers, received regular death threats, and was not above bribing local chieftains for permission to preach in their realms. Because of his own experience, he sought to end slavery, one of the first Christians to reject this practice unequivocally.

In many ways Patrick was a reluctant pilgrim: kidnapped at sixteen, sold into slavery, going against the wishes of his family and his peers, if not his own desires, to return to Ireland, where he knew he would encounter stiff resistance. Thomas O'Loughlin puts this in perspective for all spiritual pilgrims: "As part of a quest for holiness, as part of a desire to know and do the divine will, the pilgrim leaves the familiar and crosses boundaries to where he or she is not-at-home—and for pilgrims in the past this involved personal risk, for to leave one's own place was to leave behind security, recognized rights and legal protection." In Patrick's case, Ireland was "not only foreign, but indeed was the homeland of his enemies. . . . It was a place where he knew that legally and socially he was an outsider."[2]

This last statement highlights what I think is the most striking feature of Patrick's life: his willingness to forgive the very people who had enslaved him. No one at home would have blamed him had he given over to the racism of the day and condemned the Irish with derogatory slurs, packed with the extra punch of a wounded victim. But somehow, by the grace of God, he overcame the inertia of hatefulness and took up the hard work of extending forgiveness and an invitation to life to the very people who had offered him only death.

Later he would write, "I didn't go to Ireland willingly that first time—I almost died there. But it turned out to be good for me in the end, because God used the time to shape and mold me into something better. He made me into what I am now—someone very different from what I once was, someone who can care about others and work to help them."[3]

I know I'm not alone in finding it difficult to make that same offer to people who have hurt me. The temptation to hang on to the pain, to continue to blame the other, allows me to avoid looking at how I might have contributed to the problem. The lingering pain validates the emotional injury, and letting go feels too much like dismissing it. Modern Celtic writer John O'Donohue expresses the insidious nature of these wounds in his blessing poem *For Someone Who Did You Wrong*. In the poem, O'Donohue talks about a hurt that "struck outside" but then "burrowed inside," even to the point of making "tunnels" that destabilized the very ground of his confidence. After the initial blow, it would lie dormant for a while, almost as if it had done all its damage and quietly departed. But then, unexpectedly, a random thought would bring it back to life again.

The Celtic understanding of time and the rhythms of the soul acknowledges that the ability to forgive doesn't always come easily or quickly. But in time, our faith moves us toward forgiveness, not to let the other person off the hook, but to free ourselves from being enslaved to the pain of the past. We are defined not by what someone else has done to us, but rather by how all our hurts are transformed into energy to free others from similar prisons of the spirit. As the poem continues, O'Donohue becomes aware that time has brought a "new kindness" where he can acknowledge that the hurt taught his heart a kind of compassion he might otherwise have never realized.[4]

Living on the Border

My first trip to Ireland was in 1995 to visit my friend Wayne Loftin, who was serving a year-long internship with The Methodist Church in Ireland. He lived in Donegal in the far northwestern corner of the island, so the nearest large airport was in Belfast. He met my flight late one afternoon, leaving enough time to see some of the city before driving across Northern Ireland into the Republic. On the way, Wayne noted towns that had experienced bombings in the recent time of troubled relations between loyalists and those seeking independence from the United Kingdom. It was especially eerie driving through the border checkpoints, recently abandoned by the British army in a gesture to move toward more peaceful relations. A few days later, we visited Derry, a city that had suffered a disproportionate share of violence, including the "Bloody Sunday" tragedy in 1972. "It's because Derry is a border town," Wayne explained. "Border cities are where both sides feel they have the most to lose. They are volatile places."

A few years later, I was appointed to serve as senior pastor in Purcell, Oklahoma, a county seat town a few miles south of Norman. During our time there, we heard many colorful stories from the days preceding statehood in 1907. Purcell was a border town between Oklahoma Territory and Indian Territory, an attractive place for those on the wrong side of the law looking to make a quick getaway across the Canadian River.

Most of our reluctant journeys begin in times of transition, when we find ourselves living in the borderlands between health and illness, faith and doubt, comfort and discontent. Change of any kind can be unsettling, but there are some moments when we have to make a decision: Do we hunker down and hope it's all been a bad dream, or do we allow ourselves to step into a new, transformed future? I believe this is the reason so many stories in the Bible take place in border regions: The Hebrew people traversed the wilderness between Egypt and the Promised Land; the apostle Paul moved along the line between Jews and Gentiles; Mary Magdalene stood outside the empty tomb, suspended between life and death.

Jesus constantly called people into borderlands of the spirit, challenging them to let go of limitations put on them by society in order to enter into the fullness of the life of God. And it was in such a place that Jesus himself was challenged. In Matthew 15, after Jesus taught the people to attend to what was in their hearts more than they cared for outward appearances, he moved into the region of Tyre and Sidon. A quick glance at a map tells us that these were border towns between Syria and Phoenicia. With the mix of different populations and the intermingling of clashing allegiances, people here tended to be rather anxious.

It is no accident that it was here that a Gentile woman broke into the Jewish world. This is an unsettling story: A woman shrieks and publicly confronts Jesus. His first response seems rather harsh and callous. The woman begs for mercy for her daughter, who was tormented by a demon. Jesus is silent. The disciples try to brush her away. "I was sent only to the lost sheep of the house of Israel," Jesus says. The woman persists in her desperate pleas. "It is not fair to take the children's food and throw it to the dogs," he says. "Yet even the dogs eat the crumbs that fall from their masters' table," she responds. Jesus then acknowledges her great faith and heals her daughter.

A huge question hangs over this encounter: What happens when Gentiles knock on the door of Israel's God? This woman was an outsider in every way: She was a Canaanite, an ancient foe of the people of Israel. She was a Gentile, a woman, probably a single parent, and her daughter had a demon, which in that time was seen by many as a sign of divine disfavor.

This story is set on the border in every way: between old and new, male and female, Jew and Gentile, enemy and friend, the holy and the demonic. But it was the woman's brokenness, living in this in-between world, that enabled her to risk challenging such rigid boundaries and to force open a door seemingly forever closed.

We know the dangers of living in the border towns of the spirit. We want to cry out with the Canaanite woman ourselves sometimes, and we hear echoes of her cries all around us, even if issued in silence:

- from the man in the office going through a divorce who seems lost and shaken.
- from the bully on the playground who has to live with trouble at home where his cries are not heard so he acts out in the only way he knows.
- from the politician who dares to question laws and policies that further deteriorate the social fabric at the risk of alienating key constituents.
- from the young adult down the street who is suddenly withdrawn and sad.
- from the struggling mother who wants nothing more than to feed her starving children and to offer them the chance for a better future.

Border areas are places of transition, but they are also places of potential, not just of what *may* be but also of what *could* be. The Canaanite woman, and the Celts who followed in her spirit, inspire us to press ahead, especially when all seems lost, to wait with expectant hope for the desert to turn into an oasis of abundant life.

Weathering the Storms

Midway through our university study-abroad trip, we arrived in Galway on the west coast of Ireland in preparation for a short ferry ride to the Aran Islands. I will admit to being a little nervous about the ferry crossing. I was happy to see that our boat was of substantial size, but I also heard that the few miles separating the islands from the mainland were notoriously treacherous. After a few minutes, we hit the choppy waves, rocking back and forth, bouncing up and down, even going airborne at one point before slapping back on the water. A little boy threw up. We cast nervous glances toward each other and prayed that the Dramamine would do its work.

I experienced a number of emotions and questions on that short trip: What have I gotten myself into? Can we turn back? Do the regular crew members seem worried? I attempted to reassure myself, remembering that many people before me had made that trip successfully, and I tried not to think of the many who had not! It gave me renewed respect for the early Celtic missionaries who made such a difficult journey to share the gospel.

It also gave this person from a land-locked state new insight into the story of Jesus roused from sleep in a boat on the Sea of Galilee and silencing a storm, to the relief of the disciples. This story has always been a favorite of Christians. One of the earliest symbols of the church was that of a ship, securely sheltering its members from danger. The Spanish artist El Greco, known for his ability to capture the mystical, emotional essence of his subjects, painted this scene with storm clouds boiling in the distance held at bay by the outstretched arm of Jesus.

We continue to turn to this story because it speaks directly to our experience as well. There are times when we are tossed by the storms of life, where we feel out of control, overwhelmed by forces beyond our ability to manage. The fear that gripped the disciples also grasps us. We panic. We feel that God is absent, asleep at best, and wonder if God cares.

Several years ago, I was on a church mission trip to Nicaragua. Our team was dealing with the feelings of disorientation that come with being in a foreign country with its different language, food, and customs. We were there to help the local folks build a medical clinic, and many of us felt that we had few skills to contribute. We were astounded by the overwhelming need and our inadequacy to make a difference.

The spiritual leader of our trip was Don Forsman, a retired United Methodist minister. One night he began our devotional by reading the story of Jesus stilling the storm from Mark's Gospel. We knew the story, but Don focused on one little line. When Jesus first left the shore, Mark wrote, "Other boats were with him" (4:36). When Matthew and

Luke told this story, neither of them mentioned these other boats. Commentators on this text pay it little attention; it seems a throwaway line. But Don saw the presence of these accompanying boats as key to understanding this account. While the storyline follows Jesus and the disciples, other folks were there too. Others experienced the fear evoked by the unexpected storm as well as the sudden calm.

Years later, I was called upon to preside at a funeral for a man in his forties who died after a three-year battle with cancer. In reflecting on what I could say on this occasion, Don's devotional came back to me. So at the service I noted that while Gary was experiencing the pain in his body, receiving occasional glimmers of good news and buckets of bad, he wasn't alone. His family and friends were there with him, going through the same storm.

It is in these disorienting moments, when we are most vulnerable, ironically, that we find ourselves most open:

- open to the idea and possibility of change. Old habits or routines that no longer move us forward are brought into question.
- open to see what is truly of value. When we lose material goods, or relationships, or people close to us, we grieve their absence but celebrate the community that continues to support us.
- open to our common humanity. When our comfortable lives are disrupted, we find increased solidarity with others all around us who live with so much loss that our comforts had shielded from view.

When Jesus said, "Let us go across to the other side" (Mark 4:35), it seemed to be another routine request but before they even settled into the boat, a storm came up quickly. The elements arrayed against them, and us, are not so important. The nature of the storm is not important—all that matters is that Jesus is there and "other boats are with us."

Living and Dying Well: Saint Columba

Along with Patrick and Brigid, Columba served as one of the three most influential leaders who shaped the character of Christianity in Celtic lands. We have more historical information on him than other saints from this time, along with a wonderful hagiography written by Adomnán, ninth abbot of Iona and a relative of Columba, about a hundred years after the saint's death. Columba was known as a man of action and may appear out of place in a chapter on reluctant journeys, but he models positive responses to two of life's most difficult journeys: exile and death.

About sixty years after Patrick died, Columba was born in Donegal in 521. A son of the influential northern Uí Néill clan, his family noticed his courage and tenacity from a young age and believed him destined for greatness, perhaps even becoming high king of Ireland. But his heart pulled him to a life in the church. While still a teen, he joined the monastery at Clonnard to study with the famous teacher Finnian, along with three thousand other students. Even here, his abilities caused him to stand out from the crowd. His restless spirit and passionate faith drove him to be a leader in the great monastery building movement of the late sixth century. He established settlements at Durrow in the south, Kells in the midlands, and Derry on the northern coast. This last was his favorite as seen in this verse ascribed to him:

> For this do I love Derry,
> For its stillness, for its purity,
> For it is quite full of white angels
> From one end to the other.

The most significant decision in his life, however, was when he left Derry in 563 at the age of forty-two. He pushed off from shore with twelve companions in a little boat, finally settling on the small island of Iona off the coast of modern-day Scotland. His monastery there would become the center of evangelistic outreach to the Scottish mainland and northern England, the premier site for the copying of sacred texts, and a popular pilgrimage destination for people seeking spiritual enrichment and for kings needing political advice.

Theories abound on why Columba left his beloved Ireland for life on this small slip of land. The earliest witness from Adomnán indicates that he and his companions were *peregrini pro Christe*, traveling where the wind took them following the call of God. Others suggest Columba had political motives, attempting to help his family extend their territory by establishing a base north of their ancestral homeland. By modern standards, Iona is remote, requiring a ride through the Scottish highlands, boarding two ferries and a bus across an island in between them; but in ancient times, it actually was strategically located in the center of busy sea routes. Medieval scholar Máire Herbert suggests the opposite, that Columba's political connections and family wealth compromised his ability to devote himself to the religious life, and he sought a land where his motives were not questioned.[5]

The most colorful and famous account for this pilgrimage comes from a mid-twelfth-century document that recounts an incident from Columba's days as a student. His teacher, Finnian, possessed a well-known Psalter he brought back from Rome. Columba wanted a copy of this book for himself, so on his own time and with his own resources, he reproduced the document. When its existence was discovered, Finnian claimed that any copy of his book belonged to him as well. This dispute went to the high king, and in one of the first copyright cases on record, he ruled in favor of Finnian: "To every cow its calf, to every book its copy." The story goes that Columba was so upset that his family went to war to avenge his honor. They won the Battle of Cúl Dreimne but at the heavy cost of three thousand lives lost on the opposing side. Now guilt-ridden, Columba chose self-imposed exile, sailing north until coming to an island where he could no longer see his beloved homeland.

Whether Columba arrived on Iona by his own choice, as punishment for rash behavior, or by the hand of God, we know that once there, it served as fruitful ground for the ministry of this complicated and energetic man. His hagiography tells stories of tenderness, such as instructing one of the brothers to nurse a wounded crane back to health, as well as demonstrations of his holy power, including an encounter with the Loch Ness Monster where the sign of the cross sends the beast whimpering away. The versatile nature of the saint is reflected in his names. The Irish name given to him at birth, *Crimthann*, means "fox," but later he took the name *Columcille* (literally, "dove of the church") and its Latin version, *Columba*. He was just as comfortable negotiating with kings and settling disputes as he was in caring for those in need. The love his religious community held for him is reflected in these lines composed just a few years after he died:

> He numbered the stars of Heaven,
> this teacher of all things,
> this Dove, this Columcille. . . .
> Sages held him close to their hearts.
> He was our jewel. . . .
> He was sweet to listen to.
> Being a priest was but one of his
> callings.[6]

After thirty-four years on Iona, Columba sensed the time of his death approaching. Rather than cause for alarm or fear, Adomnán framed his death in the context of resurrection. During the Easter celebration, he longed to "depart to Christ the Lord," but he chose to delay his passing a little longer so as not to sadden the brothers during the festival. On a Sabbath day the following month, he made the rounds of the different areas of the monastery, making sure the barn was well stocked with supplies and climbing to a hilltop to bless the community. When he paused to rest, a white work horse ambled over to the saint, put his head on his chest, and wept tears of great mourning. Columba went next to his hut where he had been writing out a copy of Psalm 34. After transcribing the verse "They that seek the Lord shall not want for anything that is good," he put down his pen and said, "Let my successor write what follows." He attended vespers in the church, then returned to his lodgings to offer one last word of blessing to the brothers, encouraging them to love one another and to be at peace. When the bell rang for midnight prayers, Columba hurried to the church ahead of the others and knelt alone to pray before the altar. When the other brothers arrived, they found him in a much weakened state. They lifted his body and cradled his head as he died in their arms.[7]

Adomnán's stylized account of Columba's death highlights what each of us can hope when that time comes for us. He was at peace with the members of his community and with God. He made sure to provide for the physical needs of those in his care. While he faithfully attended to his work, he realized that there was a time to stop and to entrust the continuation of that ministry to the hands of another. It's telling that although he was incredibly weak at the end, he didn't die until he was in the company of his beloved community.

Unfortunately, all deaths are not as peaceful and ordered as the one experienced by Columba. Some come at the end of lingering illnesses, others suddenly and with little warning. Some die with broken relationships unmended and tragic regrets. The Celtic Christians hold before us the assurance that God walks with us on all our reluctant journeys. Even if every situation doesn't have a happy ending, we can be assured that our losses and griefs, our sorrow and anguish, will not have the last word. Even the darkest night holds the promise of transformation into life beyond what we can imagine.

John Buchanan, pastor at Fourth Presbyterian Church in Chicago for many years, recalls when his wife's older brother died. It was the first Sunday of Lent. "I was reminded," he writes, "that we were moving toward the celebration of resurrection. I thought of the radical conviction upon which our faith rests—that there is a power loose in the universe that overcomes even death.

"My wife's father died several years ago at the same time of year. She sat by his bedside on the last night, holding his hand. 'What did you do all night long?' I asked. 'What did you say?'

"'I ran out of things to say,' she explained, 'so I sang all the Easter hymns I could remember, and I said, 'Easter's coming, Daddy, Easter's coming.'"[8]

> In life, in death, in life beyond death,
>   God is with us.
> We are not alone.
>
> Thanks be to God.[9]

6

Blessings on the Journey

It was October when Ann, who would become my wife, and I had our first date. That meant that we had been together only a few weeks before the holiday party season began. We weren't sure our relationship was quite ready for the pressure attached to taking someone to a family gathering at Christmas, but we decided to go ahead anyway. It might produce some clarity to see what we were getting ourselves into.

So on a chilly afternoon in mid-December, we made the drive from Tulsa to Springdale, Arkansas, where Ann's mother's side of the family congregated at her aunt's home. We stepped into a chorus of greetings, handshakes, and hugs and acted like we didn't hear the whispered questions and curious comments about Ann's "new friend."

When we got back in the car to leave, Ann asked, "Well, how did it go?" I said, "You left me at two critical moments." The first one came not long after we arrived. While Ann was in the restroom, her aunt called everyone to dinner, then asked if I would offer the blessing for the meal. As a pastor,

I get that request frequently, but this one made me nervous. Are there some family customs of which I'm not aware? Do they always honor a certain relative of happy memory in the prayer on this occasion? Anyway, I bowed my head and said a prayer. After the amen, I looked up, a little anxiously. Everyone seemed satisfied. Ann returned just in time to grab a plate, wondering who had said the prayer.

The second moment came when we all went into the family room to open gifts. With so many people, Ann and I relinquished the chairs to the older folks and found a place on the floor near the Christmas tree. She pointed out that the gifts there were only for the children under the age of eighteen. The adults would exchange gifts later. And with that she went into the kitchen for more coffee. I learned later that she started visiting with her cousin, Paula, and lost track of the time. Meanwhile, for me, time was slowing to a crawl. Feeling a little lonely and exposed, my anxiety was broken when the children began distributing packages, some to cousins, some to siblings. I noticed that one little boy was having trouble recognizing the name on one of the tags. The person helping him took a look, then pointed toward me. Sure enough, he walked over and dropped the package in my lap—the only adult to be so honored. I looked down at the tag, thinking there had been a mistake. It read "To: Ron." Further confusion, since my name is Rod. I looked around, searching for some kind of sign or help. Then I noticed that another one of Ann's aunts, sitting on the couch behind me under her bouffant hairdo, was looking at me, as if she had been watching me for a while. She wore a benign smile and slowly nodded her head up and down, indicating that this gift did indeed belong to me. At that point, I did what any sane person would do in that situation: I got up and left the room.

In the end, I learned there had been no mistake. The aunts had scurried around to find something they could wrap just so I could have a gift to open. While it may have been a generic token, what it represented meant even more. This family, in their somewhat awkward way, was blessing me. They didn't know me, but they knew I was special to one of their loved ones, and they were determined to do all they could to make me feel welcome.

Tribal cultures place great emphasis on blessing. We see this in the Hebrew Bible where the patriarch bestowed the legacy, honor, and wealth of the family to the next generation. To seek a blessing and to receive a blessing were very important.

Blessing and cursing played a central role in pre-Christian Celtic society. Tribal poets, known as bards, skilled in composing and reciting heroic verses, were esteemed almost as highly as kings. It was believed that their songs of praise could propel a person to a life of prosperity, but woe to those who offended a member of this guild. The mere threat from a bard to compose a verse pointing out a person's evil or haughty ways was all it took for most perpetrators to straighten up their lives. The Celts thought that druids, pre-Christian religious leaders, had the power to call on spiritual forces to relieve suffering or to cause vengeance on enemies. Particular locations served as portals to otherworldly realities, so those seeking renewal

of body and spirit traveled to these sites for healing. The natural world could be the source of life
or death. Many of their rituals and holidays were
designed to keep the community in harmony with
nature.

These beliefs translated easily to Christianity. Blessings once thought to arise from magical
forces now were seen as the bounty of a benevolent God. Instead of calling on one of the gods from
their pantheon or some animating spirit to come to
their aid, they recalled the sainted lives of the ones
who once lived among them and summoned the
blessed Trinity and angelic beings to be present
with them. The Celts believed that the presence of
God infused all of nature; indeed, the essence of
God was revealed there. They readily incorporated
the Book of Psalms into their regular worship. They
were right at home with their breadth of emotion—
from exultation to despair—and the way the natural
world was integrated into the language of faith:

> O Lord, our Sovereign,
>   how majestic is your name in all the
>   earth!
>
> You have set your glory above the
>   heavens. (Psalm 8:1)
>
> The heavens are telling the glory of
>   God;
> and the firmament proclaims his
>   handiwork. (Psalm 19:1)

Their rituals, including prayer times and holidays, were redesigned to give priority to keeping

in sync with the heavenly world over the rhythm of the earthly seasons. The Celtic Christians continued to attach special significance to specific locations, but now they served as the means to recognize the sacredness of every place. As spirituality historian Philip Sheldrake writes, "Human places, natural features and landscapes are at the same time the concrete world of our daily experience in which we consciously live and yet something more. They also constitute a world of wonder, power, spirits and God."[1]

Prayers of Protection

Ancient Ireland could be a dark and dangerous place. Too many people were lost to complications of childbirth or infections that would be treated easily today. In addition, they had to deal with occasional plagues causing unbearable grief and marauding bands of cattle thieves or local skirmishes leaving behind untold casualties. While the Celts enjoyed the food and beauty nature provided, they knew only too well the drenching rain, freezing temperatures, and raging of the sea that showed a more menacing side to their environment.

Prayers from the Celtic tradition call on the powers of heaven and earth for blessings on themselves and their communities and for protection from all malevolent forces that may threaten them.

Two particular types of protection prayers feature prominently among the Celts. One was known as a *caim* (pronounced "KEY-em"), or encircling prayer. Praying in the Celtic world was a very physical act, either by kneeling, standing, or with hands lifted up. When praying a caim, the person would extend their arm and index finger while moving in a clockwise direction, repeating a prayer such as this one from the Scottish islands:

The Sacred Three
My fortress be
Encircling me
Come and be round
My hearth and my home.[2]

This action evokes the creation of a barrier—a spiritual force field, if you will—making real to the anxious person at prayer the presence of God, keeping all fears at bay. David Adam comments, "This was no magic, it was no attempt to manipulate God. It was a reminder by action that we are always surrounded by God. He is our encompasser, our encircler. It is our wavering that has put us out of tune. This is a tuning in to the fact that 'in Him we live and move and have our being.'"[3]

The second form of protection prayer from the Celtic tradition is known as a *lorica* (pronounced "luh-RYE-ka"), the Latin word for breastplate. The image comes from a suit of armor ready for battle, one that Paul evokes when encouraging the Thessalonians to "put on the breastplate of faith and love, and for a helmet the hope of salvation" (1 Thessalonians 5:8), and one the writer to the Ephesians encourages for the early Christians when he says to "put on the whole armor of God" (Ephesians 6:10-17). The most famous lorica prayer is Saint Patrick's Breastplate, with its familiar section quoted in Chapter 3, "Christ with me, Christ before me, Christ behind me." While tradition attaches Patrick's name to this prayer, it was actually written around three hundred years after his death. Its beautiful language and distinctive structure make it worthy of the saint and open a window into the Celtic understanding of their relationship with God.

The prayer begins,

> I rise today
>> with a mighty power, calling on the
>> Trinity,
>> with a belief in the threeness,
>> with a faith of the oneness
>>> of the creator of creation.

Immediately we sense a strong faith but not a personalized one. It is rooted in the theological language of the church by invoking the Trinity, understood by the Celts to represent a harmonious community of persons. Then it stretches the scope even further by referring to God as the Creator. If this prayer is intended for those who are anxious or fearful, it establishes that the person at prayer is not alone: He or she is standing in the fellowship of God the Father, Son, and Holy Spirit, even the one who created all things.

The prayer also starts by encouraging the fretful person to take action: "I rise today . . ." When we're scared, the temptation is to hide under the covers or hunker down and hope the problem resolves itself. But this prayer forces us to look beyond the fear that makes us feel weak and small by recognizing the great expanse of the physical and spiritual cosmos from which we can draw strength. Six of the prayer's eight stanzas begin with this phrase, which places the person at prayer within the greater story of the life of Jesus and the presence of the heavenly hosts and the ancestors in faith.

The fourth stanza summons the powers of God flowing through elements of the natural world: "light of the sun . . . brilliance of fire . . . firmness of earth," followed by those strengths coming through God's character in the fifth stanza: "with the words of God to speak for me, / with the hand of God to protect me."

Only after identifying, and being reassured by, all these mighty powers does the prayer turn in stanzas six and seven to naming the evil forces putting them in peril: "every cruel force which may attack my body and soul, . . . poison and burning, . . . drowning and wounding." But these terrors are flicked away with the caim prayer:

> Christ with me, Christ before me, Christ
>   behind me,
> Christ in me, Christ below me, Christ
>   above me,
> Christ to the right of me, Christ to the
>   left of me,
> Christ where I lie, Christ where I sit,
> Christ where I stand,
> Christ in the heart of everyone who
>   thinks of me,
> Christ in the mouth of everyone who
>   speaks of me,
> Christ in every eye which sees me,
> Christ in every ear which hears me.

The breastplate prayer concludes by coming full circle, returning to the first stanza, repeating it now with renewed vigor and confidence:

I rise today
> with a mighty power, calling on the
> > Trinity,
> with a belief in the threeness,
> with a faith in the oneness
> > of the creator of creation.[4]

The prayer as a whole anticipates modern insights into the dynamics associated with healing of the spirit. Whenever we are depressed due to grief or circumstances, the tendency is to turn inward, to pull all emotional resources to the core in order to survive. Fear, about dangers real or imagined, creates confusion where the slightest provocation is magnified and we become obsessed with fending off the threat at all costs. In those times of distress, we know we're on the road to wholeness when we are able to lift our heads and to look to the horizon instead of only inward, to notice the needs of others instead of exclusively our own.

Saint Patrick's Breastplate prayer relentlessly reminds us that we do not travel through the darkness alone. It speaks peace to the immobilizing emotional chaos by reconnecting us to our sources of greatest strength. Familiar reference points come back into focus as we are brought back into relationship with God, with creation, within the Christian story, within community. Everywhere we turn, Christ is there. Anytime, day or night, Christ is there. In everyone we encounter, friend or foe, Christ has already prepared the way so that each of us sees reflected in the other the very image of God.

Prayers for All of Life

In the late 1800's, the Celtic lands went through yet another time of transition. Modernization threatened the old ways of life, and an increasing number of people moved from farms to cities. Alexander Carmichael, a civil servant living in Edinburgh, feared that much of the folklore and religious practices of the past were in danger of being lost. As a native of the remote outer islands of western Scotland, he carried a deep love for the rhythmic cadences and colloquial perspectives on life in which he was immersed as a boy. So for several years, when he found some spare time and on summer vacations, he traveled through these rural areas, stopping to visit with local, everyday people, listening to their prayers and stories, collecting them for posterity. The six-volume work resulting from his efforts is called the *Carmina Gadelica*, meaning "songs of the Gaels." It consists of stories, poems, charms, customs, and, of most interest for our purposes, prayers.

Reading through this collection, it becomes apparent that the particular forms of prayer and theological emphases of the early Celtic Christians had been passed down over the centuries. The presence of God in the natural world finds vivid expression:

> There is no bird on the wing,
> There is no star in the sky,
> There is nothing beneath the sun,
> But proclaims His goodness.[5]

We hear the familiar strains of a caim prayer and the veneration of the Trinity:

The compassing of the Three be on
    thee,
The compassing of the Three preserve
    thee.[6]

Carmichael noted how the whole of life and
each part of the daily routine were proper objects
of prayer. He discovered blessings for planting
and reaping crops, for bedtime and morning, for
daily chores such as milking cows and weaving
cloth. While the ancient prayers acknowledged
the intimate connection between the spiritual and
physical worlds, these prayers went even further.
What appear to be the most mundane tasks actually are alive with ministering angels and serve as
opportunities to deepen the understanding and
practice of our faith. For example, this beautiful
thanksgiving prayer begins with echoes of Saint
Patrick's lorica, then moves to a spiritual interpretation of getting dressed and gazing out over the
morning landscape:

Thanks to thee, O God, that I have
    risen today,
To the rising of this life itself;
May it be to Thine own glory, O God of
    every gift,
And to the glory of my soul likewise.

O great God, aid Thou my soul
With the aiding of Thine own mercy;
Even as I clothe my body with wool,
Cover Thou my soul with the shadow
    of Thy wing.

Help me to avoid every sin,
And the source of every sin to forsake;
And as the mist scatters on the crest of
 the hills,
May each ill haze clear from my soul,
 O God.[7]

These words shine a convicting light on my tendency to compartmentalize my life. I'm very focused on my to-do lists for work and home: appointments to make, reports to file, shopping to squeeze in sometime, deciding what's for dinner. Too often prayer, worship, and spiritual disciplines become one more thing on the list. How would my life change if I could see *through* the to-do lists so that those tasks took on spiritual significance? Theologian John Macquarrie described the Celtic Christians as "God intoxicated" whose lives were "embraced on all sides by the divine Being. But this presence was always mediated through some finite this-worldly reality, so that it would be difficult to imagine a spirituality more down-to-earth than this one."[8]

A particularly striking prayer is for the kindling of the fire in the morning. For those of us with reliable heating units, it's hard to imagine the difficulty of maintaining a comfortable temperature in a rustic home. Most of those houses had peat fires burning in a central location. At nighttime, someone had to "smoor" the fire, covering it just enough that it smoldered without putting it out completely. In the morning, the fire had to be stoked or kindled back into flame. This could not have been a pleasant task on a cold, damp morning: to roll out of bed before anyone else and try to make the house a little more comfortable and breakfast possible. But notice how this most unhappy chore takes on new meaning when viewed through the eyes of faith:

> I will kindle my fire this morning
> In presence of the holy angels of
> heaven, . . .
> Without malice, without jealousy,
> without envy,
> Without fear, without terror of any one
> under the sun,
> But the Holy Son of God to shield me.

What a way to start the day! Instead of complaining about being cold and why everyone else got to sleep a little longer, this prayer begins with a reminder that this routine, but important, task was not done anonymously. The holy angels of heaven were already waiting so that the day would begin with a blessing. While stoking the fire, instead of thinking about yesterday's problems and the present day's challenges, the prayer purges all that would hinder good relationships with others and calms anxieties.

Then the prayer transforms the physical act into a spiritual one:

> God, kindle Thou in my heart within
> A flame of love to my neighbor,
> To my foe, to my friend, to my kindred
> all, . . .
> From the lowliest thing that liveth,
> To the Name that is highest of all.[9]

Even as the smoldering embers grow into a blaze, may love catch fire and spread in my heart toward enemies as well as friends and family. Nothing is to be overlooked or taken for granted; everything is to be tended with the same watchful attention given the fire. Who knew that such a rich, spiritual meaning could come from a simple household chore?

Can it be that all of life is sacred? Can we see God in our morning routine while fighting with the copier, taking notes in class, driving to work, in line at the grocery store; when loving, arguing, and reconciling with those closest to us; when going to sleep and waking?

Prayers that draw from tasks common to an agricultural society such as smooring fires and plowing fields may seem remote to our experience, but the pattern works just as effectively when applied to our modern world. For example, driving a car falls into the routine category for most people. Depending on our mood and the driving skills of those on the road with us, the car is certainly a place of prayer, although not always with the most reverent intentions! Inspired by the Celtic tradition, Carole Parker imagined how this commonplace activity would be transformed if instead of focusing on what the other guy was doing or rushing to our destination we saw the drive as a blessing:

> Bless the car to me, O Lord
> Bless me to my car.
> Be in my driving
> Be in my concentration
> Be in my decisions.

Bless this journey to me, O Lord.
It is a small reflection of my journey
    through life,
My life given to you.
My way chosen by you.
A journey with you
A journey to you.
A journey to knowing myself
A journey to knowing you
A journey of being saved and healed.

Bless the people I drive by, O Lord.
May they be aware of you in this place.
Bless the owners of these businesses.
May they deal justly and honestly.
Bless the schools, polytechnics and
    universities.
Give a teachable spirit to both pupil
    and teacher.[10]

The prayers that sustained the Celts through the seasons of life carried them over the threshold of death as well. Death was not seen as the snuffing out of life or the end of a journey. Instead, it was understood as the transition to an even richer existence. This last liminal space would not be one of fear but one in which a life lived in constant communion with God would find its fulfillment. As one prayer chanted at the bedside of a dying person put it:

Thou goest home this night to thy
    home of winter

To thy home of autumn; of spring, and
of summer;
Thou goest home this night to thy
perpetual home,
To thine eternal bed, to thine eternal
slumber. . . .

The shade of death lies upon thy face,
beloved,
But the Jesus of grace has His hand
round about thee;
In nearness to the Trinity farewell to thy
pains,
Christ stands before thee and peace is
in His mind.

Sleep, O sleep in the calm of all calm,
Sleep, O sleep in the guidance of
guidance,
Sleep, O sleep in the love of all loves;
Sleep, O beloved, in the Lord of life,
Sleep, O beloved, in the God of life![11]

Blessings

For a few years, my good friend Janet Boone
coordinated the activities and maintenance needs
of the university chapel where we worked. It was
a very busy place hosting academic classes, three
weekly worship services, regular lunch and dinner meetings, weddings, recitals—the list goes on.
Managing tight schedules and changing room set-
ups involved a lot of people, most of whom were
very busy with other duties. In spite of these stress-
ful situations, everyone seemed to be very cheerful

when they came to the chapel to do their work. At some point, they usually gravitated to Janet's office where I would hear laughter break out on a regular basis.

What made things work so smoothly, and the people happy to do it, was that Janet practiced a ministry of affirmation. She made a point of saying, "Thank you," and "You always do such a good job." After a big event, she sent an e-mail to everyone involved complimenting each person and department. She got to know student workers, members of the housekeeping crew, professors—no one was outside her circle of care.

In other words, Janet was practicing the ancient art of blessing. It wasn't just a matter of acknowledging what someone did; she was affirming who they were, a person created and loved by God and cherished by their community.

Reading through the prayers of the Celts, you notice that they almost never ask God for anything directly. Instead, they recognize that God is already present and active all around them, and they call for those blessings to be made real in their own lives.[12]

This view of the presence of God in all things has a profound effect on our spirituality. If we believe that God is active in everything, even the most mundane, we are not so pressured to hit a spiritual home run every time we seek to encounter God, to believe that we have to have a mountaintop emotional experience in order to be in the presence of the holy.

We see this repeatedly in the pages of Scripture. Abraham was sitting in the door of his tent by the oaks of Mamre, cooling himself during the heat of the day, when he saw three strangers approaching who would change his life, and ours, forever. Moses was tending sheep on the side of a mountain when he noticed something that looked like a bush on fire. Hannah was celebrating a religious festival in Jerusalem as she had done many times before, silently praying, when the priest Eli told her that she would bear a longed-for son. And we see it outside the pages of the Bible as well. John Wesley was in the hull of a ship returning to England after a disastrous mission to the Georgia colony when he noticed the peace of the Moravians in the midst of a storm. And Rosa Parks was just trying to get home from work when she sat down on a bus and changed America.

As I was learning about the Celtic practices, I realized that I was not doing a good job of blessing my own family. When dropping off my children at school, "See you later" suddenly seemed an inadequate parting sentiment. So I changed that to say, not necessarily in the same order, "I love you, God bless you, have a good day." I will admit it was sometimes awkward to say and to hear such intimate words, but the children were getting the blessing anyway.

Who are those in your life you need to bless? How can you acknowledge and give thanks for those dear to you, or to those who give your life meaning, by offering a good word, a quick note of appreciation, or an act of generosity?

Of course, the opposite of blessing is cursing. Ian Bradley notes how many evils listed in the middle stanza of Saint Patrick's Breastplate involve harm done by the spoken word—incantations, spells, lying.[13] While we might not attach magical powers to words, as did the Celts, there is no denying the fact that words can encourage, and they can damage. Electronic social media amplifies their effect. Sharing inspirational messages and words of support can make someone's day. On the other hand, the anonymity or distance created by these platforms allows people to say things they would never say in person. Racial slurs, ethnic stereotypes, and just plain meanness appear in too many website comments sections. Cyberbullying and name-calling, the modern version of cursing, wreck reputations and demoralize innocent victims. Do we really want to be known as those who are masters of the put-down? Does it really make us feel better to gripe and complain, whether or not we know all the facts or actually talk to the person involved? This blessing from the *Carmina Gadelica* is just as relevant for surfing the web as for community gossip:

> The love and affection of heaven be
>   to you . . .
> Each day and night of your lives,
> To keep you from haters, to keep
>   you from harmers, to keep you
>   from oppressors.[14]

As we have seen, the Celtic Christians were very much aware of how our bodies and hearts could be broken. Diseases, natural disasters, victimization by thieves, war, and abuse created deep wounds in the human spirit. But their belief in the essential goodness of everyone compelled them to see the image of God shining through even the ones most broken by life's circumstances.

The story of Jesus feeding the five thousand as told in their beloved Gospel of John captures this Celtic perspective (John 6:1-14). Large crowds kept following Jesus until they found themselves in a mountainous area, away from restaurants and grocery stores. The question arose of how they would feed so many. The disciples found a boy who had five barley loaves and two fish, a meager amount to say the least. Jesus blessed the bread and broke it, then served the bread and the fish to the people. After everyone had all they wanted, Jesus said to the disciples, "Gather up the fragments left over, so that nothing may be lost." On the surface, it appears that Jesus was concerned about what to do with the leftovers. But the word John used is very specific: the scraps that remained were not called "trash"; they were "fragments"—broken pieces.

Perhaps John had the Crucifixion in mind, when Jesus' body would be broken. Or perhaps the people themselves are represented by the bread. John mentions that the people followed Jesus because they saw what he did for the sick, and they certainly qualified. They followed because their lives were incomplete. Some were falling apart, while others bore the burden of illness or troubled relationships. They were broken by life's demands and oppressive systems.

The fragments appeared worthless, but Jesus did not ignore them. In his hands they were blessed—transformed.[15]

The Community of Hope Christian fellowship in Tulsa was founded with the mission of reaching out to the dispossessed and marginalized, the people who often didn't feel welcomed by the church. Because they were a new congregation, they looked for some object, a symbol or a logo, that would help identify their purpose. Despite their best efforts, they could not find anything that signified their message. One day the pastor was in a pottery shop when a strange looking chalice caught her eye. Instead of a smooth cup at the top, it was misshapen, and there was what looked like a collar partially wrapped around it. When she asked the owner of the shop about this strange design, he said, "Oh, when the potter was firing this piece it broke, but instead of discarding the fragmented pieces, he just put them together to create a new one." At that moment, the pastor realized that she was holding the symbol for the new fellowship: a chalice that represented all those broken people who would come and find wholeness in their encounter with Christ.

In the tenth century, Symeon the New Theologian wrote,

> . . . and everything that is hurt,
>   everything
> that seemed to us dark, harsh,
>   shameful,
> maimed, ugly, irreparably
> damaged, is in Him transformed
> and recognized as whole, as lovely,
> and radiant in His light
> we awaken as the Beloved in every
>   last part of our body.[16]

Stephanie Paulsell tells the story of one of her friends who as a teenager suffered from terrible acne:

> She remembers a day when her anguish over the appearance of her face made her feel unable to leave the house. Seeing her distress, her father asked if he could help by teaching her a new way to bathe. Leading her to the bathroom, he leaned over the sink and splashed water over his face, telling her, "On the first splash, say 'In the name of the Father,' on the second, 'in the name of the Son,' and on the third, 'in the name of the Holy Spirit.' Then look up into the mirror and remember that you are a child of God, full of grace and beauty."[17]

The Celts would have immediately recognized this father's blessing of his daughter. It is physical, intimate, and Trinitarian, and it recognizes the beauty of God shining through our imperfections. The Celtic Christians were concerned with the healing of wounded spirits through the intimacy of soul friendships, constant prayer, and acts of hospitality. Their example teaches us to be intentional in blessing one another at every opportunity and to receive those blessings that come at surprising times and in unexpected places.

One afternoon when our son, Carus, was in elementary school, he was working on his homework at the kitchen counter while I prepared dinner. We were having a favorite family recipe for oven-roasted potatoes, one that called for a 450-degree oven. A lot of noise filled the air: I was listening to the news on the radio and thinking about all the chores yet to be done while Carus asked questions that required more than a yes or no answer. Needless to say, I was somewhat distracted when I reached into the oven to retrieve the pan of potatoes, and I touched the back of my thumb to the hot rack. Fortunately, I didn't say any bad words, but instinctively I grabbed my thumb and started jumping up and down due to the pain. I turned my frustration on Carus and chided him for talking to me at such a critical time. He looked at me wide-eyed for a moment, and then he spoke. You might have expected him to say, "Sorry, Daddy. Are you all right? Can I help you, Daddy?" But no. What he said was, "I didn't know you could jump!"

At that moment, my nine-year-old son blessed me. He looked past my misplaced anger and bestowed a measure of forgiveness far more than I deserved. He invited me to turn my mourning into dancing—literally—by tapping into that timeless stream of grace always flowing with rivers of living water.

Benediction

The Maker's blessing be yours
on your road
on your journey
guiding you, cherishing you.

The Son's blessing be yours
wine and water
bread and stories
feeding you, challenging you.

The Spirit's blessing be yours
wind and fire
joy and wisdom
comforting you, disturbing you.

The Angels' blessing be yours
on your house
on your living
guarding you, encouraging you.

God's blessing be ours;
the blessing of pilgrims
all the nights and days
of our journey home.[18]

Endnotes

Chapter 1: Embarking on the Journey

1. J.J. Ó'Ríordáin, *Irish Catholics: Tradition and Transition* (Dublin: Veritas Publications, 1980); pp. 24–25.
2. Martin Wallace, *The Celtic Resource Book* (London: The National Society / Church House Publishing, 1998); p. 62.
3. John Claypool, "Beginning in the Middle," sermon preached at Princeton Theological Seminary's Institute of Theology, June 28, 1988. I transcribed this portion from a cassette recording I have of the sermon.
4. *Celtic Daily Prayer: From the Northumbria Community* (San Francisco: HarperCollins, 2002); p. 19.

Chapter 2: Friends on the Journey

1. Kenneth Leech, *Soul Friend: The Practice of Christian Spirituality* (San Francisco: Harper & Row, Publishers, 1977); p. 42.
2. *The Wisdom of the Desert: Songs from the Desert Fathers of the Fourth Century*, translated by Thomas Merton (Boston: Shambhala Publications, Inc., 1960); p. 142.
3. *Conferences of John Cassian*, Conference 16, Chapter 3, translated by C.S. Gibson. From *Nicene and Post-Nicene Fathers, Second Series*, Vol. 11, edited by Philip Schaff and Henry Wace (Buffalo, NY: Christian Literature Publishing Co., 1894). Revised and edited for New Advent by Kevin Knight: *http://www.newadvent.org/fathers/350816.htm*.
4. *The Wisdom of the Desert: Songs from the Desert Fathers of the Fourth Century*; p. 50.
5. *Martyrology of Oengus the Culdee*, quoted in Edward Sellner, *Stories of the Celtic Soul Friends: Their Meaning for Today* (Mahwah, NJ: Paulist Press, 2004); p. 7.
6. From the article "Saint Ita" at *http://thenunsgarden.org/saint-ita.php* and "St. Ita of Killeedy: Foster Mother of the Saints of Ireland" at *http://catholicfire.blogspot.com/2015/01/st-ita-of-killeedy-foster-mother-of.html*.

7. *The Book of Discipline of The United Methodist Church, 2012* (The United Methodist Publishing House, 2012); pp. 76–78.

8. Rueben P. Job, *Three Simple Rules: A Wesleyan Way of Living* (Nashville: Abingdon Press, 2007); p. 10.

9. Anne Lamott, *Grace (Eventually): Thoughts on Faith* (New York: Riverhead Books, The Penguin Group, 2007); pp. 28–29.

Chapter 3: Markers on the Journey

1. Attributed to Saint Columba, quoted in Martin Wallace, *The Celtic Resource Book* (London: The National Society / Church House Publishing, 1998); p. 56.

2. Winston Churchill, the prime minister's speech on the House of Commons rebuilding, October 28, 1943, Cambridge, The University Press, 1944: *http://hansard. millbanksystems.com/commons/1943/oct/28/house-of-commons-rebuilding*.

3. The Celtic holidays are pronounced *Imbolc* (IM-bulg), *Beltaine* (BEY-all-TIN-ah), *Lughnasa* (LOO-nuh-sah), and *Samhain* (SOW-in [sow as in cow]).

4. Dorothy C. Bass, *Receiving the Day: Christian Practices for Opening the Gift of Time* (San Francisco: Jossey-Bass Publishers, 2000); pp. 17–18.

5. *Receiving the Day*; pp. 17–18.

6. *Selections from Ancient Irish Poetry*, translated by Kuno Meyer (London: Constable & Co., Ltd., 1911); p. 27.

Chapter 4: Hospitality on the Journey

1. I learned that the building we saw was the City Hall. This impressive structure, opened in 1906, has towers at the four corners and a copper dome, reminiscent of Saint Paul's Cathedral in London.

2. Robert C. Dykstra, *Discovering a Sermon: Personal Pastoral Preaching* (St. Louis, MO: Chalice Press, 2001); p. 138.

3. Martin Wallace, *The Celtic Resource Book* (London: The National Society / Church House Publishing, 1998); p. 90.

4. Lisa M. Bitel, *Landscape with Two Saints: How Genovefa of Paris and Brigit of Kildare Built Christianity in Barbarian Europe*, (New York: Oxford University Press, 2009): pp. 178–179.

5. Quoted by Rita Minehan in *Rekindling the Flame: A Pilgrimage in the Footsteps of Brigid of Kildare* (Kildare, Ireland: Solas Bhríde Community, 1999); p. 40.

6. This is one of many versions of this prayer.

7. Henri J.M. Nouwen, *Reaching Out: The Three Movements of the Spiritual Life* (Garden City, NY: Doubleday & Company, Inc., 1975); p. 51.

8. *The Celtic Resource Book*; p. 69, adapted.

9. "The Evernew Tongue," as quoted in *Celts and Christians: New Approaches to the Religious Traditions of Britain and Ireland*, edited by Mark Atherton (Cardiff: University of Wales Press, 2002); p. 188.

10. Toni Morrison, *Beloved* (New York: Alfred A. Knopf, 1987); pp. 87–89.

Chapter 5: Reluctant Journeys

1. *Saint Patrick's Confession*, translated by Philip Freeman, *The World of Saint Patrick* (New York: Oxford University Press, 2014); p. 24.

2. Thomas O'Loughlin, "Patrick the Missionary" in *Celtic Theology: Humanity, World and God in Early Irish Writings* (New York: Continuum, 2000); p. 44.

3. *Confession*, translated by Philip Freeman, *St. Patrick of Ireland: A Biography* (New York: Simon & Shuster, 2004); p. 184.

4. John O'Donohue, *For Someone Who Did You Wrong* in *To Bless the Space Between Us* (New York: Doubleday, 2008); pp. 172–173.

5. Noted by Ian Bradley in *Columba: Pilgrim and Penitent* (Glasgow: Wild Goose Publications, 1996); p. 22.

6. Quoted by Edward Sellner in *Stories of the Celtic Soul Friends: Their Meaning for Today* (Mahwah, NJ: Paulist Press, 2004); p. 137.

7. *Life of St. Columba*, Book III:23, translated by Richard Sharpe (New York: Penguin Books, 1991); pp. 225–229.

8. John M. Buchanan, "Easter's Coming" in *The Christian Century*, March 15, 2013, Vol. 130, No. 6: *http://www.christiancentury.org/article/2013-02/easter-s-coming*.

9. "A New Creed," The United Church of Canada, 1969: *http://www.united-church.ca/beliefs/creed*.

Chapter 6: Reluctant Journeys

1. Philip Sheldrake, *Living Between Worlds* (Boston: Cowley Publications, 1995); p. 81.

2. Quoted in Ian Bradley, *The Celtic Way* (London: Darton, Longman & Todd Ltd., 2003); p. 47.

3. *The Celtic Way*; p. 47.

4. All quotes from Saint Patrick's Breastplate in this section are from Philip Freeman's translation *St. Patrick of Ireland: A Biography* (New York: Simon & Schuster Paperbacks, 2004); pp. 161–164.

5. From "Jesu Who Ought to Be Praised" in Alexander Carmichael, *Carmina Gadelica* (Edinburgh: Floris Books, 2006); p. 45.

6. From "Encompassing" in *Carmina Gadelica*; p. 221.

7. "Thanksgiving" in *Carmina Gadelica*; p. 198.

8. John Macquarrie, *Paths in Spirituality* (New York: Harper & Row, Publishers, 1972); pp. 122–123.

9. "Blessing of the Kindling" in *Carmina Gadelica*; p. 93.

10. *http://www.rejesus.co.uk/site/module/celtic_spirituality/P6/*. Retrieved October 30, 2014. © copyright rejesus 2002 to 2015.

11. "The Death Dirge" in *Carmina Gadelica*; pp. 312–313.

12. *The Celtic Way*; p. 42.

13. Ian Bradley, *Celtic Christian Communities: Live the Tradition* (Kelowna, BC Canada: Northstone Publishing, 2000); pp. 65–66.

14. "Blessings" in *Carmina Gadelica*; p. 256.

15. This perspective on the feeding of the five thousand in John comes from Flora Slosson Wuellner, "A Broken Piece of Barley Bread" in *Weavings*, XIX:6, November/December 2004; pp. 6–12.

16. Symeon the New Theologian, 949–1022 A.D., taken from *The Enlightened Heart: An Anthology of Sacred Poetry,* edited by Stephen Mitchell (New York: Harper & Row, 1989); pp. 38–39.

17. Stephanie Paulsell, *Honoring the Body: Meditations on a Christian Practice* (San Francisco: Jossey-Bass, 2002); p. 48.

18. From the Leaving Service, pp. 28–29, *Iona Abbey Worship Book* (2009), Iona Community, Wild Goose Publications, Glasgow, *www.ionabooks.com.*

Celtic Christianity Timeline

Date	Key Persons
400	**Pelagius** (360–430) arrives in Rome
432	**Patrick** (390–461) returns to Ireland
470	**Brigid** (452–524) establishes Kildare
520	**Finnian** (470–549) establishes Clonard
548	**Ciaran** (516–549) establishes Clonmacnoise
560	**Brendan** establishes Clonfert (484–577)
563	**Columba** (521–597) establishes Iona
585	**Columbanus** (543–615) travels to France
590	**Kevin** (498–615) establishes Glendalough
635	**Aidan** (600–651) establishes Lindisfarne in Northumbria
650	**Cogitosus** writes *Life of Brigid*, beginning the writing of hagiographies
657	**Hilda** (614–680) establishes Whitby
684	**Cuthbert** (634–687) elected abbot of Lindisfarne
731	**Venerable Bede** (673–735) publishes *Ecclesiastical History of the English People*
867	**John Scottus Eriugena** (810–877) completes the *Periphyseon*

Note: Some of these dates are disputed but are reliable as close approximations.

Key Events and Artwork

410—Romans leave Britain

mid-sixth century—monasteries spread out of river plains to all areas

664—Synod of Whitby

700—*Lindisfarne Gospels*

750—Ardagh Chalice

793—Viking raids begin at Lindisfarne

eighth & ninth centuries—high crosses built

800—*Book of Kells*

tenth century—*Voyage of Brendan*

Pronunciation Guide

This guide offers approximate pronunciations, some of which may vary according to regional dialects.

General Terms

Anamcara	ah-nahm-CAR-ah
Caim	KEY-em
Carmina Gadelica	car-MEEN-ah gah-DEL-i-kah
Celt	KELT
Chronos	CROW-nohs
Currach	KER-rah
Exagoreusis	ek-ZAG-or-E-oo-is
Hagiography	hog-e-OG-rah-fy
Hesychia	hess-e-SHE-ah
Hiraeth	HERE-eth
Hospites mundi	hos-PIT-es MOON-di
Kairos	KYE-rohs
Lorica	luh-RYE-kah
Peregrini	pair-eh-GREEN-ee
Peregrinus	pair-eh-GREEN-us
Perichoresis	pear-i-core-E-sis
Syncellus	sin-SILL-us

People and Places

Adomnán	AD-om-non
Aidan	AY-din
Aran	AIR-in
Boudica	BOO-di-kah
Brigid	BRIJ-id
Broicsech	BROCK-sheh
Clonmacnoise	klon-mac-NOIS
Clonnard	klo-NARD
Columcille	kol-um-KILL
Coroticus	ko-ROT-i-kus

Crimthann	KRIM-than
Cuchullian	koo-HULL-in
Cúl Dreimne	kool DREM-nah
Dubthach	DUB-ach
Glendalough	GLEN-dah-lock
Grianan Ailligh	ga-REE-ah-non AH-leeg
Iona	eye-O-nah
Maeve	MAYV
Monasterboice	MON-as-ter-bois
Muiredach	MWIH-rah-dock
Pelagius	pel-AY-jee-us
Uí Néill	oo-e NEIL

Celtic Holidays

Imbolc	IM-bulg
Beltaine	BEY-all-TIN-ah
Lughnasa	LOO-nuh-sah
Samhain	SOW-in (sow as in cow)

Select Bibliography

General Overview

A History of the Irish Church 400–700 A.D., John
R. Walsh & Thomas Bradley. Blackrock, Co. Dublin:
Columba Press, 2005.

Good, general overview of early Celtic Christianity with special attention to Patrick, monasticism, peregrini, and penitentials.

*How the Irish Saved Civilization: The Untold
Story of Ireland's Heroic Role from the Fall of Rome
to the Rise of Medieval Europe*, Thomas Cahill. New
York: Anchor Books, 1995.

Engaging, sweeping overview of historic Celtic Christianity with attention to earlier Celtic stories and mythology written for a general audience.

*In Search of Ancient Ireland: The Origins of the
Irish from Neolithic Times to the Coming of the
English*, Carmel McCaffrey and Leo Eaton. London:
Rowman & Littlefield, 2002.

This companion to the PBS series of the same name gives a good overview of Irish history and how Christianity developed in that setting.

The Celtic Way, Ian Bradley. London: Darton,
Longman & Todd Ltd, 2003.

Solid introduction to the theology, history, and practice of Celtic Christianity.

History and Art

Life of St. Columba, Adomnán of Iona, translated and with an introduction by Richard Sharpe. New York: Penguin Books, 2005.

Considered a model of modern scholarship in the translation of this classic hagiography from the seventh century of Columba, with extensive notes and an introduction covering Columba's life and legend.

Discovering Saint Patrick, Thomas O'Loughlin. Mahwah, New Jersey: Paulist Press, 2005.

Translations of primary documents relating to Saint Patrick, with extensive annotations and a solid introduction to his life. Somewhat technical, but an excellent resource.

St. Patrick of Ireland: A Biography, Philip Freeman. New York: Simon & Schuster Paperbacks, 2004.

Very readable, general overview of Patrick's life and ministry by a classics scholar with attention paid to different aspects of Irish society of the time.

The Book of Kells: An Illustrated Introduction to the Manuscript in Trinity College Dublin, second edition, Bernard Meehan. London: Thames & Hudson, 1995.

A detailed overview of this important illuminated manuscript of the four Gospels, with several full-color photos.

The World of Saint Patrick, Philip Freeman. New York: Oxford University Press, 2014.

A wonderful collection of primary sources including Patrick's writings, *The Life of Saint Brigid*, and *The Voyage of Saint Brendan*.

Spirituality and Theology

Iona Abbey Worship Book, The Iona Community. Glasgow: Wild Goose Publications, 2001.

Liturgies in the Celtic spirit for general services and for special services such as for healing and creation from a leading group in the Celtic revival.

Living Between Worlds: Place and Journey in Celtic Spirituality, Philip Sheldrake. Boston: Cowley Publications, 1995.

Excellent treatment of how symbols and places meld with spirituality in the Celtic world.

Listening for the Heartbeat of God: A Celtic Spirituality, J. Philip Newell. Mahwah, New Jersey: Paulist Press, 1997.

Discusses how different persons from the Celtic tradition serve the common theme of carefully listening to God.

The Celtic Way of Prayer: The Recovery of the Religious Imagination, Esther de Waal. New York: Doubleday, 1997.

Creative treatment of Celtic themes such as journey, time, and saints, using prayers from the *Carmina Gadelica*.

The Path of Celtic Prayer: An Ancient Way to Everyday Joy, Calvin Miller. Downers Grove, Illinois: InterVarsity Press, 2007.

This popular evangelical author introduces six forms of prayer inspired by the Celtic tradition with suggestions on how to practice each one.

The Soul of Celtic Spirituality: In the Lives of Its Saints, Michael Mitton. Mystic, Connecticut: Twenty-Third Publications, 1996.

The author chooses one aspect of fourteen different Celtic saints, both famous and obscure, as a window into the spirituality of this tradition. Each chapter ends with questions for reflection and discussion, a suggested Bible reading, and a prayer.

To Bless the Space Between Us: A Book of Blessings, John O'Donohue. New York: Doubleday, 2008.

A collection of creative blessing prayers for different stages of life inspired by the Celtic tradition.

Fiction

Absolution by Murder, Peter Tremayne. New York: Penguin Group, 1997.

This is the first in a series of murder mysteries by the author set in early Medieval Ireland. The central character is Sister Fidelma, a qualified *dalaigh*, or advocate of the law courts. These books provide a sense of that time in history and religious and legal practices.

Some of these works are out of print or difficult to find. Most can be accessed through used book outlets and interlibrary loan.